YOU CAN NEGOTIATE ANYTHING

Herb Cohen

BANTAM BOOKS

TORONTO · NEW YORK · LONDON · SYDNEY · AUCKLAND

YOU CAN NEGOTIATE ANYTHING
*A Bantam Book / published by arrangement with
Lyle Stuart Inc.*

PRINTING HISTORY
*Lyle Stuart edition published November 1980
9 printings through August 1981*

*A Selection of Book-of-the-Month Club, Playboy Book
Club, McGraw-Hill Book Company, Preferred Choice
Bookplan and US Book Club.*

*Serialized in New York Times Syndication,
Book Digest Magazine, Family Circle and
Computer Decisions Magazine.*

*Bantam edition / February 1982
11 printings through May 1987*

ISBN 0-553-25999-7

Published simultaneously in the United States and Canada

Bantam Books are published by Bantam Books, Inc. Its trademark,
consisting of the words "Bantam Books" and the portrayal of a
rooster, is Registered in U.S. Patent and Trademark Office and in
other countries. Marca Registrada. Bantam Books, Inc., 666 Fifth
Avenue, New York, New York 10103.

PRINTED IN THE UNITED STATES OF AMERICA

20   19   18   17   16   15   14   13   12   11

In memory of my father, Morris Cohen, whose negotiating strategy was always to give much more than he received. His life spoke an eloquence of its own.

Contents

Our best thoughts come from others.
                    —Ralph Waldo Emerson

Acknowledgments

This book, like any other, has a long ancestry. Many people and experiences have shaped my thinking over the years. In this respect, it is honest and accurate to say that work on this manuscript began a long time ago.

Despite this qualification, what follows is primarily the product of thirty years of direct involvement in thousands of negotiations. During this period, I have profited immensely from working with many distinguished thinkers and doers, in both government and the private sector.

However, I would be remiss if I did not specifically mention some individuals who contributed to my development. Though they cannot be held responsible for anything I have written, their names follow: Robert E. Alberts, Saul D. Alinsky, Renee Blumenthal, Harlan Cleveland, Michael Di Nunzio, Viktor E. Frankl, Jay Haley, Eric Hoffer, Eugene E. Jennings, George F. Kennan, Marya Mannes, Norman Podhoretz, Bill Rosen, Bertrand Russell, Arthur Sabath, Francis A. Sinatra, and of course, Esther Greenspun.

To others, who left their mark on these pages, I extend my appreciation—specifically George Elrick, Eleanor Harvie, Anita Lurie, and my best friend, Larry King. I am indebted to Carole Livingston for her advice and to my publisher, Lyle Stuart, for his unique blend of risk taking and patience.

Above all, I want to thank my life partner and wife, Ellen, for her involvement and support. This undertaking would not have even been contemplated, let alone completed, without her.

Before you go any further, let me elaborate upon three things that you will notice as you proceed.

First, I wish to assure the majority of my readers that I intend no slight in using the masculine tense predominantly. In writing this book, I spent endless hours trying to grapple with the semantic bias of the English language. My initial attempts to eliminate the pronoun problem resulted in prose that was either confusing or clumsy. Consequently, you may occasionally come across a bit of verbal sexism. When this occurs, accept my apology. Obviously, I do not believe that because Eve was fashioned from Adam's rib, women are a side issue. In this age of emancipation, the fault lies primarily in our fatherland's mother tongue.

Second, I have chosen not to furnish any footnotes, references, or technical texts to support the concepts or ideas in this book. My purpose was not to produce a scholarly work for the specialist, but to write a practical and readable guide for laypeople. The thoughts and examples must make sense on their own. If they don't, even a divine footnote cannot provide salvation.

Third, I have "painted with a broad brush," so you will not become mired in technicality or legalese. This was done to make it easy to understand the broad underlying concepts. Obviously, in some instances I have made suggestions tongue in cheek, in a figurative sense—not to be taken literally.

It is not my intention to prescribe behavior or tell you what you should want. Instead, my aim is to illuminate your reality and its opportunities. In doing so, I will point out thinking and behavior that may be limiting you, as well as options and alternatives from which you can choose. Each of you will then, within your own comfort and belief system, have a way of getting what you want, based on your unique needs.

H.C.

Northbrook, Illinois
September 1980

PART ONE

YES, YOU CAN

*To get to the Promised Land you have to
negotiate your way through the wilderness.*

1. What is negotiation?

Your real world is a giant negotiating table, and like it or not,
you're a participant. You, as an individual, come into conflict with others: family members, sales clerks, competitors,
or entities with impressive names like "the Establishment" or
"the power structure." How you handle these encounters can
determine not only whether you prosper, but whether you can
enjoy a full, pleasurable, satisfying life.

Negotiation is a field of knowledge and endeavor that fo-
cuses on gaining the favor of people from whom we want
things. It's as simple as that.

What do we want?

We want all sorts of things: prestige, freedom, money, justice, status, love, security, and recognition. Some of us know
better than others how to get what we want. You are about to
become one of these.

Traditionally, rewards presumably go to those possessing
the greatest talent, dedication, and education. But life has dis-

illusioned those who hold that virtue and hard work will triumph in the end. The "winners" seem to be people who not only are competent, but also have the ability to "negotiate" their way to get what they want.

What is negotiation? It is the use of information and power to affect behavior within a "web of tension." If you think about this broad definition, you'll realize that you do, in fact, negotiate all the time both on your job and in your personal life.

With whom do you use information and power to affect behavior off the job? Husbands negotiate with wives, and wives with husbands. (I hope your marriage is a collaborative Win-Win negotiation.) You use information and power with your friends and relatives. Negotiations may occur with a traffic cop poised to write a ticket, with a store reluctant to accept your personal check, with a landlord who fails to provide essential services or wants to double your rent, with the professional who bills you for part of the cost of his or her education, with a car dealer who tries to pull a fast one, or with a hotel clerk who has "no room," even though you have a guaranteed reservation. Some of the most frequent and frustrating negotiations occur within a family, where parents and children often unknowingly engage in this activity. Let me give you an example from my personal experience.

My wife and I have three children. At nine, our youngest son weighed fifty pounds, remarkably light for a child his age. Actually, he was an embarrassment to our entire family. I say that because my wife and I like to eat, and our two oldest children have voracious appetites. Then there was this third kid. People would ask us, "Where did he come from?" or "Whose kid is that?"

Our son arrived at his emaciated state by developing a life strategy of avoiding vicinities where food might be served. To him "meals," "kitchen," "dinner," and "food" were profane words.

Several years ago, I returned home on a Friday evening

after an ascetic week of travel and lectures. It's lonely on the road—at least for some of us—so I pondered a potential negotiation with my wife later in the evening. As I entered our home, I was dismayed to find my wife curled up in a fetal position on the couch, sucking her thumb. I perceived that there might be a problem. "I've had a rough day," she murmured.

To snap her out of her doldrums, I said, "Why don't we all go to a restaurant for dinner?"

She and our two oldest replied in unison, "Wonderful idea."

The nine-year-old dissented. "I'm not going to any restaurant! That's where they serve food!" At this point I lifted him bodily and carried him to the automobile, which is one type of negotiation.

As we entered the restaurant, the nine-year-old continued to complain. Finally he said, "Dad, why do I have to sit around the table with everyone? Why can't I be *under* the table?"

I turned to my wife. "Who'll know the difference? We'll have four around and one under. We may even save money on the check!" She was against this at the outset, but I convinced her that the idea might have merit.

The meal began, and the first ten minutes were uneventful. Before the second course arrived, I felt a clammy hand creeping up my leg. A few seconds later my wife jumped as though she'd been goosed.

Angry, I reached under the table, grabbed the culprit by his shoulders, and slammed him down on the seat beside me. I muttered, "Just sit there. Do *not* talk to me, your mother, your brother, or your sister!"

He replied, "Sure, but can I stand on the chair?"

"All right," I conceded, "but just leave all of us alone!"

Twenty seconds later, without warning, this lean child cupped his hands around his mouth and shouted, "This is a crummy restaurant!"

Startled though I was, I had enough presence of mind to grab him by the neck, shove him under the table, and ask for the check.

On the way home, my wife said to me, "Herb, I think we learned something tonight. Let's not ever take the little monster to a restaurant again."

I must confess that we never *have* offered to take our lean child to a restaurant again. What our nine-year-old did on that embarrassing occasion was to use information and power to affect our behavior. Like so many of today's youngsters, he's a negotiator—at least with his parents.

You constantly negotiate at work—though you may not always be aware you're doing it. Subordinates or employees use information and power to affect the behavior of those above them. Let's say you have an idea or proposal you want accepted. What's required is that you package your concept in such a way that it meets the current needs of your boss, as well as the present priorities of your organization. There are many people with technical expertise who lack the negotiating skill needed to sell their ideas. As a result they feel frustrated.

In today's world a wise boss always negotiates for the commitment of his employees. What is a boss? Someone with formal authority who attempts to get people to do voluntarily what must be done. You and I know that the best way to shaft a boss these days—to transform him into a shaftee with you being the shaftor—is to do precisely what he or she tells you to. When told what to do, you write it down and ask, "Is *this* what you want?" Then you proceed to comply, literally.

Two weeks later, your boss runs up to you and blurts, "What happened?"

You reply, "I don't know. I did exactly what you told me to do."

We have a name for that in today's world. We call that phenomenon "Malicious Obedience." And there are many people out there who practice it to a refined art. So if you happen to be a boss, you never want an employee to do exactly what you tell him to do. You want him to occasionally do what you *don't* tell him to do . . . often what you *can't* tell him to do, because many problems can't be anticipated.

Not only do you negotiate with your boss or your subordinates, but you also negotiate with your peers. To get your job done, you need the cooperation, help, and support of many people whose boxes aren't situated beneath yours on an organization chart with the arrows pointing upward. These people may have different functions or different disciplines. They may even be in different parts of town. You need negotiation skill to obtain their help and support.

You may negotiate with customers or clients, bankers, vendors, suppliers, even governmental agencies from the Internal Revenue Service to the Occupational Safety and Health Administration. You may negotiate for a larger budget, more office space, greater autonomy, time off from work, a geographical transfer, or anything you believe will meet your needs. The point I'm making is that you negotiate more often than you realize. Therefore you should learn to do it well. You can learn to be effective—and thus enhance the quality of your life—on and off the job.

In every negotiation in which you're involved—in every negotiation in which I'm involved—in fact, in every negotiation in the world (from a diplomatic geopolitical negotiation to the purchase of a home)—three crucial elements are always present:

1. *Information.* The other side seems to know more about you and your needs than you know about them and their needs.
2. *Time.* The other side doesn't seem to be under the same kind of organizational pressure, time constraints, and restrictive deadlines you feel you're under.
3. *Power.* The other side always seems to have more power and authority than you think you have.

Power is a mind-blowing entity. It's the capacity or ability to get things done . . . to exercise control over people, events, situations, and oneself. However, all power is based on perception. If you think you've got it, then you've got it. If you think you don't have it, even if you have it, then you don't have it. In short, you have more power if you believe you have power and view your life's encounters as negotiations.

Your ability to negotiate determines whether you can or can't influence your environment. It gives you a sense of mastery over your life. It isn't chiseling, and it isn't intimidation of an unsuspecting mark. It's analyzing information, time, and power to affect behavior . . . the meeting of needs (yours and others') to make things happen the way you want them to.

The fine art of negotiation isn't really new. By my definition, two of the greatest negotiators in history lived approximately two thousand years ago. Neither man was part of the Establishment of his time. Neither had formal authority. However, both exercised power.

Both men dressed shabbily and went around asking questions (thereby gathering information), one in the form of syllogisms, the other in the form of parables. They had objectives and standards. They were willing to take risks—but with a sense of mastery of their situation. Each man chose the place and means of his death. However, in dying, both gained the commitment of followers who carried on after them, changing the value system on the face of this earth. In fact, many of us try to live by their values in our daily lives.

Of course, I'm referring to Jesus Christ and Socrates. By my definition, they were negotiators. They were Win-Win ethical negotiators, and they were power people. In fact, both of them deliberately used many of the collaborative approaches I will teach you through this book.

The sign wasn't placed there
by the Big Printer in the Sky.

2. Almost everything is negotiable

Information, time pressures, and perceived power often spell the difference between satisfaction and frustration for you. Using a hypothetical situation, let me illustrate. You awaken one morning and go to the refrigerator for a glass of milk. You plan to drink most of it straight, then pour the rest into your coffee. As you open the refrigerator door and grasp the container, you're aware that it's clammy. Stepping back, you notice a pool of water on the floor. You call your spouse over to diagnose the situation, and your spouse gives you the technical name for the problem: "Broken refrigerator."

You comment, "I think we need a new one. Let's buy it at a 'one-price store,' where we won't be hassled." Because your children are too young to be left alone, you tell them, "Get in the car. We're going to buy a refrigerator." En route you discuss your cash-flow problem. Since you're not very liquid at the moment, you decide to spend no more than $450.00

for the acquisition. In other words, you have a firm objective in mind.

You arrive at the one-price store: Sears, Ward's, Gimbel's, Marshall Field's, Macy's, Hudson's, or whatever. For the sake of the narrative we'll say it's Sears. You walk briskly to the Large Appliances Department, with your organization trailing behind you. As you run your eye over the refrigerators, you see one that appears to meet your needs and specifications. However, as you approach, you notice that on the top of this model is a sign reading, "Only $489.95"—$39.95 more than your checking account can handle. It's no ordinary sign scrawled with a Magic Marker. It's symmetrical and professionally done: block-printed on expensive chipboard. And it appears to have been placed there by the Big Printer in the Sky.

You call out, "Hello, there!" and a salesperson ambles over.

"Yes . . . may I help you?"

You reply, "I'd like to chat with you about this refrigerator."

He says, "Do you like it?"

"I certainly do," you admit.

He says, "Good . . . I'll write up the sales slip."

You interject, "No . . . wait—maybe we can talk."

He arches an eyebrow and says, "When you and your wife finish discussing this, you'll find me in Hardware," and strolls away.

Now I ask you, will this be an easy or a difficult negotiation? Most people in our culture would say difficult. Why? Because of the great imbalance in information, apparent time pressure, and perceived power.

Information. What do you know about the salesman's needs or the store's needs? Is the salesman on salary, commission, or a combination of both? You don't know. Does he have a budget, a quota, or a deadline? You don't know. Has he had a great month, or did his boss warn him to sell a refrigerator today "or else"? You don't know. What's the inventory situation on this model? Is it the store's hottest item, currently on backorder, or is it a dog the store manager will dump at any price? You don't know. What are the itemized costs on this model? You don't know. Is the store making a profit on this model? If so, how much? You don't know.

Obviously, you don't know very much about the salesman or the store. But does the salesman know something about you? Yes. He knows you're interested in the refrigerator. People may browse in the Sporting Goods, Clothing, or Stereo Departments at Sears, but not in the Large Appliances Department. They examine refrigerators when and because they need them. Over and above this "given fact," the salesman knows which nearby competitors sell refrigerators, whether they're featuring special sales at present, and how much they're charging.

Though he may—for the moment—seem to be ignoring you and your spouse, he's actually listening to your conversational exchanges with a cocked ear. He hears you discussing your old refrigerator, your cash-flow problem, and your need for a new refrigerator. Almost anything you and your spouse say furthers the informational imbalance and strengthens the salesman's hand.

Little comments like: "The color really *is* just right" . . . "I don't think we'll be able to beat this price at Ward's across the street" . . . and "The freezer compartment is the roomiest I've seen" give the salesman a growing edge.

Note that the salesman never responds directly to any question that might give *you* information. His response to any question is a counter-question. If you ask, "I'm not saying I'll buy this refrigerator, but if I do, when do you think you could deliver it?" he'll say, "When would you like it delivered?" When you reply, "How about early this afternoon?" he'll say, "Why so soon?" At that point one of you will comment, "Because we have about seventy dollars' worth of food spoiling rapidly."

Does the salesman like this information? Yes, because you've exposed your deadline to him without knowing his.

Time. Compounding the expanding informational gap is the problem of organizational pressure and time. The salesman you're dealing with seems relaxed. His organization isn't visible. How about your organization? It's very visible, but it's not united. The wife says, "Let's go." The husband says, "Let's stay," or vice versa.

What about the two children you brought into the store with you? Where are they? Are they beside the refrigerator, at parade rest, quietly waiting for the sale to be consummated? No. One youngster is playing hide-and-go-seek in the refrigerators.

"Where is he?"

"I think he's in the yellow one . . . the one with the door closed. If we don't get him out in three minutes, he'll suffocate!"

Where's the other kid? At the far end of the store with a hockey stick and a plastic puck, shooting slap shots against washers and dryers. Every few minutes he shouts, "Come on! Hurry up! The game is starting!"

While your organization is putting the screws to you, the appliance salesman wanders around acting as though he is almost totally disinterested in selling that refrigerator. Periodically he carelessly says, "Hi, there. Make up your mind?" as though he were passing on his way to pluck a mango or a papaya.

Power. In addition to all this, there's the problem of power. Power, in this instance, manifests itself in two forms:

A. *The power of precedent.* Most people firmly believe that they can't negotiate with a one-price store. If I ask them why, they're likely to reply, "Why else would they call it a one-price store? This results in the following chain of cause and effect.

1. They're convinced they can't negotiate with a one-price store. . . .
2. Therefore, they don't *try* to negotiate with a one-price store . . .
3. . . . which results in their inability to negotiate with a one-price store, proving they were right to begin with.

This is a prime example of creating a self-fulfilling prophecy.

Have you ever observed someone make a half-hearted attempt to bargain with a one-price store? The approach itself contains the seeds of failure.

The customer walks up to the sign indicating the price and points to it timidly. Of course, the salesman knows the customer's intent, since he's been through this scenario many times. But he wants the customer to say the words.

The salesman finally asks, "What's the problem?"

The customer just points to the sign and mumbles, "You know."

The salesman says, "Is something wrong with the sign?"

The customer stammers, "No, no . . . it's just the pr . . . pr . . ."

The salesman innocently asks, "The what?" and the customer finally blurts, "The price!"

At this point, the salesman adopts his righteous indignation pose and states, "Please, sir, this is Sears!"

If this ever happens to me, I respond apologetically, "Oh . . . I'm sorry. I didn't realize where I was!" at which point my wife turns on her heel and starts to walk out of the store, remarking over her shoulder, "I'm never going shopping with you again!"—which, by the way, is not all that bad, because I've accomplished a collateral objective in the process.

There's a way to break out of this bind: Don't act as though your limited experience represents universal truths. It doesn't. Force yourself to go outside your own experience by vigorously testing your assumptions. You'll discover, to your astonishment, that many of them are false. Raise your aspiration level. Avoid the negative attitude portrayed in the following jingle:

> *They said 'twas a job that couldn't be done;*
> *He half-heartedly went right to it.*
> *He tackled that job that "couldn't be done" . . .*
> *And by George, he couldn't do it.*

As a negotiator, take some risk, break free from the precedent of your past experiences, challenge your assumptions, raise your aspiration level, and increase your expectations.

While you and your spouse are confronting that $489.95 sign in the store, there's another form in which power is manifesting itself:

B. *The power of legitimacy.* The power of legitimacy is power derived from perceived or imagined authority—often authority that's represented by something inanimate, such as a sign, a form, or a printed document—normally, authority that isn't questioned.

For instance, if I were to suggest that you do something, you would evaluate my request based upon your needs. If my request and your needs matched, you might comply. But if a sign directed you to do something, your chances of complying would be virtually guaranteed. Let me emphasize that point with an example.

If you travel at all, you're familiar with a little sign behind each Holiday Inn's registration desk, plus a still smaller sign posted on each room's door. Both signs read: "Check-out time is 1 P.M."

What percentage of guests do you think inconvenience themselves by literally checking out by 1 P.M.? Someone once asked me that question. I pondered for a moment and replied, "Forty percent." I subsequently learned, from Holiday Inn executives, that the figure is roughly between ninety and ninety-five percent, depending on the motel's location.

Does that figure startle you? It did me. Fifty-five percent of Americans vote in a good year, but ninety-five percent check out by the Holiday Inn check-out time. The question is, what causes this lemming-like migration of ordinarily independent people to the cashier at the appointed hour?

Five years ago, I happened to be at a Holiday Inn. Because I had to catch an early afternoon flight, I walked toward the cashier at 12:30 P.M. in order to pay my bill and leave. The lobby was empty. At that moment I felt a slight hunger pang, so I decided to get the buffet luncheon, put it on my bill, and return. After eating, I glanced at my watch. The hands indicated 1 P.M. Since there'd been no one at the cashier's cage before, I assumed there'd be no more than three people there now.

When I got to the lobby I noted twenty-eight people lined up before the cage, like prison inmates waiting to be fed. I couldn't believe it. How was it possible to progress from zero to twenty-eight in a half hour? I mused: "These probably aren't guests checking out. Chances are, from their appearance, they're out-of-towners on a guided tour of the area's facilities. Part of the tour must consist of showing them this Holiday Inn." That being the case, I wasn't going to wait in a line that obviously was not mine. I decided to bypass the sightseers, walk up to the cashier's cage, and form the *real* check-out line.

As I moved forward, passing these "tourists," several of them glanced at me—but not with love. Awareness hit me. Slightly embarrassed, I tried to appear nonchalant as I positioned myself at the rear of the line.

Once there, I tapped the shoulder of the person in front of me and asked, "What's the line for?"

He replied, "Check-out."

"How come?"

"Check-out time, that's how come," he mumbled.

"How'd you *know* about it?" I asked.

"I read it on my door, that's how I knew."

That was a very significant comment. He saw it emblazoned on a door, and that's why he was there.

A second example of the power of legitimacy: A subordinate in a business organization whips up the nerve to walk into the boss's office and says, "Excuse me, but I'd like a raise. I really feel I deserve a raise."

Does the boss reply, "No, you can't have a raise"? Never. Instead he says, "You certainly deserve a raise. However . . ." ("However" is synonymous with "Strike that!") He shuffles papers aside, points to a printed card positioned under glass on the desk, and quietly states, "It's unfortunate that you're at the top of your pay grade."

The subordinate mutters, "Oh . . . I forgot about my pay grade!" and backs off, aced out of what might rightfully be his by printed words. In effect, the subordinate says to himself, "How can I possibly argue with a printed sheet positioned under glass?"—which may be precisely what the boss *wants* him to say.

A third example of the power of legitimacy: Twenty years ago I was involved in the legal end of real estate. People came to me to sign their leases and have them countersigned. Most paid their security deposits and moved along without reading the forms. On rare occasions someone would say, "I'd like to read this lease before signing it. I have a constitutional right to do so!"

I'd always reply, "Of course you have a right to do so. Go right ahead and read it!"

Halfway through the form the person would exclaim, "Wait a second! Hold it! This document practically makes me an indentured servant for the duration of the lease!"

I'd reply, "I doubt that. This is a standard form. There's the form number in the lower left corner."

The person usually responded, "Oh . . . a standard form. Well, in that case . . ." and he or she would sign, bullied into submission by several printed digits that apparently possessed some magical property.

In rare cases where a person still hesitated to sign his or her name, I might add, "The legal people won't approve of any changes." Keep in mind that the legal people didn't even *know* they wouldn't approve of any changes. Nevertheless, the phrase worked like a charm, since "legal people" projects, on a wide screen, a powerful image of legitimacy. One theoretically doesn't fool around with the legal people.

Meanwhile, back at the Sears outlet, you stand staring at that $489.95 sign, overawed by supposedly unchallengeable power, as were the people at the Holiday Inn, the subordinate asking for a raise, and the people signing leases. Yet in none of the situations should you be overawed. Every one of the situations is negotiable.

How can I say that? Because almost anything that's the product of a negotiation has got to be negotiable, including the price on the sign above the refrigerator.

Think about it for a moment. How did Sears come up with the $489.95 figure? You know as well as I do. The marketing people said, "Let's make it $450.00. That'll move a lot of refrigerators."

The financial people said, "Prudence dictates that when we sell a refrigerator it should be at a profit. Make that $540.00."

The advertising people interrupted and said, "Psychological studies indicate that the best number is $499.95."

Someone else impatiently said, "Look, we have a business to run. Can't we get together on this?"

They did. They compromised. They got together and came up with the $489.95. There was no Big Printer in the Sky.

Some things are not the product of a negotiation. The Ten Commandments was not a negotiated document. It's certainly difficult to negotiate with the Lord when he presents you with a *fait accompli* etched in stone. The Sermon on the Mount was not a negotiated document. Christ didn't get together with his followers and say, "Give me your input. We'll form a task force. Break up into subcommittees and work something out." Since these items are "sacred givens," they're in a different category from the Sears price, Holiday Inn's check-out time, the pay grade, and even the standard lease.

Because so many things *are* negotiable doesn't mean that you or I should negotiate all the time. If you were to ask me, "Do you negotiate with one-price stores? Do you negotiate with Sears?" I'd be perfectly frank with you and reply, "One of my life strategies is never to go into Sears."

My point is, whether you do or don't negotiate anything should be strictly up to you, based on your answers to the following questions:

1. Am I comfortable negotiating in this particular situation?
2. Will negotiating meet my needs?
3. Is the expenditure of energy and time on my part worth the benefits that I can receive as a result of this encounter?

Only if you, as a unique individual, can answer yes to all three of these questions should you proceed to negotiate. You should always have a sense of mastery over your situation. Pick and choose your opportunities based upon your needs. Don't allow yourself to be manipulated or intimidated by those who aren't concerned with your best interests.

You have the freedom to choose your attitude toward any given set of circumstances and the ability to affect the outcome. In other words, *you can play a much greater role than you thought in shaping your life and improving your lifestyle.*

*The secret of walking on water
is knowing where the stones are.*

3. Getting your feet wet

Let me reconstruct the scenario. You, your spouse, and your two children are at a Sears store confronted by a refrigerator whose asking price is more than you can afford to pay. Yet you want that refrigerator. Is it worth negotiating for? If your answers to the three questions that closed the last chapter were yes, you should proceed full speed ahead. But how? What can you say and do?

Generating competition

To begin with, don't define yourself too narrowly. Don't regard yourself as someone who wants to buy a refrigerator. Regard yourself as someone who wants to sell money. *Money* is the product that's up for sale. The more people there are who want your money, the more your money will buy. How do you get people to bid for that money? You generate competition for it.

Staying with the Sears situation, a foolproof way to generate competition for your money is to inform the salesman that rival outlets have a comparable model at a lower price. The fact that rival outlets are eager to accept your money gives you instant leverage . . . as does the fact that Sears is often in competition with itself. You find it astonishing that Sears can compete with itself? Just examine the catalogue displayed in the same store. There, right in the middle of a large-appliances page, is the same refrigerator for $440.00 plus a $26.00 delivery charge. Show that page to the salesman, then start negotiating.

Satisfying needs

You have other options, and they pivot on the satisfaction of your needs, real or fictionalized. In a fundamental sense, *every* negotiation is for the satisfaction of needs. Sears presents you with a $489.95 asking price that meets *its* needs . . . but what about yours? After all, you're the other party in the transaction. Ideally, both parties should win, or come out ahead, when a transaction is consummated.

There are several ways you can snap the Sears salesman into a keen awareness of your needs. You can ask, "What colors does this model come in?" If the salesman replies, "Thirty-two," you say, "What are they?" When he finishes telling you, you exclaim, "That's *it?* Those are the *only* colors you have?"

When he says, "Yes. Just what are you looking for?" you explain, "We have a psychedelic kitchen. These colors are much too square. They'd clash! I hope you'll make some adjustment in the price."

A second way to express your needs is to discuss the refrigerator's icemaker. You comment, "I notice this model comes with a built-in icemaker."

The salesman replies, "Yes, it does. It'll make cubes for you twenty-four hours a day, for only two cents an hour!"

(Note that he's made a totally unwarranted assumption about your needs.)

You counter this false assumption by saying, "That presents a difficult problem. One of my kids has a chronic sore throat. The doctor says: 'Never any ice! Never!' Could you possibly remove the icemaker?"

He retorts, "But the icemaker's the whole door!"

You say, "I know . . . but what if I promise not to use it? Shouldn't that affect the price?"

A third way to express your needs—and your dissatisfaction with the refrigerator's features—is to discuss its door. You can say, "This model swings open from the left. My family's right-handed." Comments like this indicate to the salesman that your needs aren't being met fully. Therefore, *his* needs shouldn't be totally satisfied.

Going on sale

You can also ask, "When is it going on sale?" or "Did I miss the sale?" The assumption is that, if it's not currently on sale, it either will be or just was. There's no earthly reason why you should be penalized for awkward timing.

"A little blemish here!"

An extremely effective option you can employ is the old floor-model technique. The floor-model technique has two aspects. With aspect number one, you walk up to the refrigerator, examine it intensely while the salesman stares at you, and mutter, "I notice a little blemish here!"

The salesman replies, "I don't see anything."

You persist, "There seems to be a little nick . . . a tiny blemish on the side. In fact, as the light hits it, I notice there are multiple blemi on the side of the refrigerator. Is there no multiple blemi discount?"

What if there are no multiple blemi on the refrigerator?

You can always *make* blemi. (I'm not covering ethics now. I'm dealing with options, even if I'm doing it tongue in cheek.) Remember the kid with the hockey stick and the puck? Have him work on his slap shot closer to the refrigerator.

Aspect number two of the floor-model technique is known as the ITD, short for internal-trauma discount. The implication is that there *must* be imperfections within a floor model. Perhaps they're not visible to the naked eye, but they're there. After all, people have been opening and closing that refrigerator's door and fingering its trays and compartments for months. The floor model's like a street walker who's been around the block several times: one of the walking wounded, suffering from the internal stress of being manhandled. Because of this, you're entitled to an internal-trauma discount, or standard ITD.

Off-tackle slant

You can always move off the major item under discussion and deal with a secondary element related to the total price. Conceivably, the salesman is limited in how much he can reduce the actual cost of the primary item, but he may have more flexibility and "give" in other areas, such as a trade-in allowance.

Therefore, you can say, "Well, if that's your price, I'd like $150 for trading in my present refrigerator. It's in excellent shape."

If the salesman says, *"What . . . ?"* you interject, "All right . . . I'll make that only $50 off."

Now I concede you may not often do this with refrigerators, but people successfully use this approach when buying cars.

What if . . . ?

Another extremely effective option at your disposal is the use of the words "What if?" "What if?" is a magic phrase in negotiations. For example: What if I buy four refrigerators? Will that affect the price? What if *I* take it home in a pick-up truck, instead of having *you* deliver it? Will that affect the price? What if I buy a washer-dryer and a waffle iron at the same time? Will that affect the price? What if over the next six months, our neighborhood syndicate buys one refrigerator a month? Will that affect the price?

You may not always get precisely what you want when asking "What if . . . ?" but nine out of ten times, the person you're dealing with will make a counter-offer in your favor.

Don't forget that although the posted $489.95 price was arbitrarily arrived at, many things are buried in that figure, including installation, delivery charges, service contract, and warranty, all of which cost Sears money. If you can save Sears any or all these expenses, the store should kick the savings back to you. For example, if you ask the salesman, "Does that price include an installation charge?" and he replies, "Yes, it does," you then comment, "Good . . . I have a set of tools at home. I can make any necessary connections and adjustments myself."

The ultimatum

Supposing your time is limited and you don't feel like negotiating. You approach the first salesman you see and say, "Look . . . you want to sell this refrigerator, and I want to buy it. I'll give you $450.00 right now, take it or leave it."

When you turn on your heel and walk away, will the salesman follow you out to the street? Nope, I don't think so. Why? Because he has nothing whatsoever invested in a relationship with you or in the overall transaction. Furthermore, he resents your curt approach. The key to making an ultimatum prevail is always the extent to which the other side makes an investment of time and energy.

Keeping this principle in mind, let's try another way. You casually walk into the Large Appliances Department at two o'clock on a Monday afternoon when floor activity is at a minimum. You say to the salesman, "I'm interested in seeing your entire line of refrigerators!" From two to four have him show you every model on the floor, explaining all the benefits.

Finally you remark, "Before I make up my mind, I'll have to come back tomorrow with my spouse."

The salesman has now wasted two hours of his time on you.

On Tuesday, again at two o'clock, you arrive with your spouse. You seek out the same salesman. You repeat the process of examining every model on the floor. Finally, you say to him, "Before we make up our minds, we'd like to come back with a refrigerator engineering specialist: my mother-in-law. She knows a lot about these things. See you tomorrow afternoon!"

The salesman now has four hours invested in you.

On Wednesday, at the appointed hour, you walk into the department with your spouse and mother-in-law. You induce the salesman to repeat his demonstrations till four, at which time you mumble, "Hmmmm . . . know what? I can't quite make up my mind!"

The salesman now has six hours of his life invested in you.

On Thursday afternoon, as expected, you walk in alone and say, "Hi there—remember me? I'm interested in buying a refrigerator."

The salesman will make a wry face and say, "I should hope so!"

You continue, "Look . . . I only have this $450.00 plus a book of matches, a fountain pen, and eight cents in change. I just love this model. Please . . . maybe we can make a deal." Then if he doesn't respond immediately, you shrug, pivot, and slowly start for the exit.

Will the salesman follow you? Yes. He has an investment in the situation, and he wants some return on the effort he has expended. He'll probably mutter, "Okay, okay! Enough is enough. It's a deal."

Why does he *take* your "Take it or leave it" offer (though you didn't use those words)? Because you've set up your ultimatum in such a way that its acceptance is virtually guaranteed. You've made the ultimatum palatable and have forced the salesman to spend an inordinate amount of time with you. He's doing a cost-benefit analysis of the situation and inwardly groaning, "I've got six hours invested in this meatball! But the devil known is better than the devil unknown. Who knows what else is lurking out there on the street?"

The nibble

The tactic known as the "nibble" works on the same basis. You may not be familiar with the term, but when I describe it you'll experience a shock of recognition. In this example, I'm going to assume, for ease of reference, that you're a man. But the same situation can apply to a woman. Just mentally switch the frame of reference from that of a men's clothing store to that of a dress shop or boutique.

You enter an exclusive men's shop in the downtown area of where you live, to buy a suit. Someone important to you is getting married, and you want to look good at the wedding. Because men's lapel widths change from year to year, owing to planned obsolescence, you're concerned about style. That's why you have a tape measure in your pocket.

"May I help you?" asks a salesman.

"I think so . . ." you reply, frowning thoughtfully.

For three and a half hours you shuffle from rack to rack and from suit to suit, painstakingly measuring lapels, always trailed by the salesman, who doesn't dare leave because you keep asking questions about shoulder widths, pocket flaps, sleeve styles, cuffs, and number of buttons. You repeat, over and over, "How long will this particular suit stay in style?" When he offers his educated guess, you ask, "Are you *sure?*"

After you've examined thirty-nine suits and fingered seventy-eight lapels, and the now stony-faced salesman is ready to "blow his cool," you say, "I think I'll take that Hickey-Free-man for $370.00—that one over there . . . the one with the very subdued stripes."

The salesman sighs with relief. Trying to remain calm, he murmurs, "Would you follow me, please?" He leads you into the small mirrored room in the rear where the store's tailor does alterations. You remove the suit you're wearing, slip into the Hickey-Freeman you're about to purchase, and stand on a special wooden box before a three-way mirror. Near you, while you stand on the box, is the salesman, now somewhat relaxed as he writes up the sales slip and calculates his com-mission.

Beneath you, as you teeter back and forth on the platform, an elderly gentleman with a stooped back, pins in his mouth, and a tape measure around his neck is on one knee. He re-moves five pins from his mouth and slides them into the material. Moments later, he makes chalked X's on the seat of the pants, then tugs in three inches at the crotch. As he does this, he mumbles in an accent you can't identify, "This is a beautiful suit. It hangs well on you." Wherever you go that old guy always has an accent. Maybe it's not an accent—just the pins in his mouth.

At this juncture, you twist your head toward the salesman and ask, matter-of-factly, "And what kind of tie will you be throwing in free?"

The salesman stops writing. He looks at the old man on the floor. The old man raises his head, not knowing whether to shove in another pin and make another chalk mark. He releases your crotch. The whole thing swings forward three inches.

That is what's known as the "nibble."

What goes on in the salesman's mind after the first wave of hatred subsides? He grunts inwardly, "This blankety-blank has consumed three and a half hours of my time. I didn't have a coffee break. I've strained both shoulders putting thirty-nine jackets on his back. I've watched the nitwit measure seventy-eight lapels. All right; that's down the drain. What have I got here? What can I assemble from the wreckage? A $370.00 sale, from which I'll get a $60.00 commission. For the sake of the $60.00, I suppose I can take $7.00 from my pocket and buy this clown a tie wholesale. I just hope I never see him again!"

Will you get that tie? Of course. Will you win the love and admiration of the salesman? That's something else again. He will give you a free tie because of his emotional involvement in the situation, not because of his affection for you.

Would the nibble have worked if he *hadn't* invested an inordinate amount of time? No. The success of a nibble is in direct proportion to the amount of time invested. No time investment, no dice. That's why you should always induce the other side to invest in a situation. And that's why your initial approach to a negotiation should always be collaborative, as though you're hungry for help.

Help me

Acting as though you're hungry for help is the opposite of acting like you know it all. What do I mean by acting like you know it all? Consider some top executives in private industry, and even in government. Because of popular mythology that dictates how they should look and act, these leaders strive to project an impressive image.

This image is an artful cosmetic job. It's a blend of Robert Redford or Robert Goulet on a good day, laced with a dash of Lorne Greene as commander of the spaceship *Battlestar Galactica* (or, better still, on the Ponderosa, with Hoss, Little Joe, and Adam galloping behind him). This stereotyped executive is slightly gray at the temples, though he has a full head of smartly styled hair. His jaw is square and thrust forward. His voice is deep and resonant. His handshake is firm enough to crush your knuckles. He strides about with his virile walk. ("Hi, there! Top executive striding about!") He always rumbles, "Good to see you!" whether he means it or not.

If you awaken this plastic executive in the middle of the night, after he's been drinking and partying excessively, he'll leap out of bed and exclaim, "Hi, there! Top executive getting up! Good to see you!"

If you then ask him, "Tell me, top executive, have you ever had a pimple?" he'll reply, "Huh?" You see, he's never *had* one!

This hollow, stereotyped model is a fraud. He's for the birds, because it's self-defeating (and also tiring) to forever stride about, straight-backed and dignified, bursting with expertise and knowledge. It's self-defeating to pretend to always know everything. But it's periodically beneficial to say the equivalent of, "I dunno . . . help me!" Admitting that you don't have all the answers humanizes you and causes others to be more receptive to your approach.

Weakness as a strength

In negotiation, dumb is often better than smart, inarticulate frequently better than articulate, and many times weakness can actually be strength. So train yourself occasionally to say, "I don't know," "I don't understand," "You lost me some time ago," or "Help me," when these phrases suit your purposes.

Think of your own experiences when dealing with stupid people. What happens to all your sophisticated arguments, logic, and comprehensive data when you're dealing with a moron who can't even comprehend what you're talking about? Obviously, your persuasive devices are worthless.

Have you ever tried to negotiate with someone you perceive has a learning or speaking disability? For example, imagine that I'm trying to negotiate with you and that you stammer or stutter or pretend to. I might say, "Okay, what's your objection to making this deal?"

You reply, "Num . . . num . . . num . . ."

I say, "Take it easy. What are you trying to say?"

You reply, "Num . . . num . . . num . . ."

I say, "Does that mean number one?"

You nod yes.

"All right, what *is* number one?"

You reply, "The pri . . . pri . . . pri . . ."

I say, "Does that mean the price?"

You nod yes.

"All right, now we're rolling. What's number two?"

You reply, "The qua . . . qua . . . qua . . ."

I say, "Does that mean the quality?"

You nod yes . . . and so on.

What have you said? Nothing. What am I doing? I'm helping you with your argument, and I'm investing time in the situation, which really puts you in control: "in the catbird seat," as card sharks say when playing with a stacked deck.

My wife claims that when I speak to blind people, I always raise my voice. Why? Unconsciously, I guess I'm trying to help them see!

Weakness itself can even result in negotiating leverage. Supposing a large bank calls a major client to express dismay over a delay in repayment of an outstanding loan. The debtor replies, "I'm really glad to hear from you, because our financial situation has recently deteriorated. In fact, the only chance of avoiding bankruptcy is for you to reduce the interest rate to prime, or prime plus one and a half percent, and defer payments on the principal for at least a year." The very helplessness of the debtor's position undercuts the power and bargaining ability of the creditor.

"We don't understand"

Especially when dealing with different regions or cultures, language is often used as a phony disability. I'm keenly aware of this because many years ago I saw three Japanese gentlemen, representing JAL (Japan Air Lines), use this ruse when dealing with a large group of sophisticated executives from an American corporation.

The company's presentation to the Orientals was overwhelming. Starting at eight in the morning, it lasted two and a half hours. With the aid of flip charts, elaborate computer printouts, and other presentation-supporting data, three projectors flashed Hollywood-style images on the screen, justifying the asking price. I was there at the conference-room table, and let me tell you, it was like Disneyland.

Throughout this dog-and-pony show, the Japanese gentlemen sat quietly at the table and said nothing.

Finally, his face glowing with expectation and self-satisfaction, one of the key American executives flicked the room lights back on and turned to the impassive men from Japan. "Well . . . what do you think?"

One of the Japanese smiled politely and answered, "We don't understand."

The blood drained from the executive's face. "What do you mean, you don't understand? *What* don't you understand?"

Another of the Japanese smiled politely and answered, "The whole thing."

I was studying the frustrated executive, and I thought he'd have a coronary. "From when?" he asked.

The third Japanese gentleman smiled politely and answered, "From when the lights went out."

The executive leaned against the wall, loosened his expensive tie, and groaned dispiritedly, "Well . . . what do you want us to do?"

All three Japanese now replied, "Can you do it again?"

Who was in the catbird seat now? Who was kidding *whom?* How could anyone possibly repeat a two-and-a-half-hour presentation with anything resembling the initial enthusiasm and conviction? The corporate asking price swirled down the drain.

Moral: Don't be too quick to "understand" or prove your intellect at the outset of an encounter. Watch your listen-talk ratio. Learn to ask questions, even when you *think* you might know the answers.

Furthermore, if you approach others asking for help, it tends to set the climate for a mutually beneficial relationship. At the least, you'll cause the other side to make an investment that ultimately accrues to your advantage.

Making the ultimatum stick

In some of the illustrations discussed earlier, ultimatums were used. Ultimatums are commonly employed, whether by a parent giving a child the "last and final proposal" regarding a curfew or by a union approaching the wire in collective bargaining.

For your ultimatum to succeed, it must meet four criteria:

1. *Frosting on the cake.* The other side must have no other choice or they must have such an investment that they can't fold their cards and walk away. Therefore, an ultimatum *must* come at the end of a negotiation, never at the beginning. You can't frost a cake until you bake it.

2. *Soft and palatable.* The words used must never belittle or offend the other side. "Hard" ultimatums, such as "Take it or leave it!" or "It's this or else!" are self-defeating. "Soft" ultimatums are palatable because they're simply a statement of your reality. Example: "I certainly understand your predicament. Your position is valid, but this is all I've got. Help me."

3. *A recipe that can't be tampered with.* It's always wise to back up your final position with some form of documentation or legitimacy. Example: "You deserve what you're asking for. I wish I could give it to you, but this is all I have in my budget!"

The visual display of the "official budget," which consists of black marks on white paper, usually does the trick. Other references, such as "This would be a violation of the presidential wage guidelines," "The F.T.C. won't let us," or "It would be against company policy" are also highly effective.

Even without supporting documentation, all of us have been swayed by such statements as, "But all my *friends* are going!" or "If we let *you* do it, *everyone* will want to do it!"

4. *Selection from a limited menu.* Never leave the other side without alternatives. Never state, "It's this or nothing!" Rather, structure the situation to allow them to make the choice with one option obviously much more desirable to them—at least compared to the other.

For instance, assume I'd like to hire you for a position in my organization. You want a $50,000 salary, but I can't afford to pay you more than $30,000. Do I say the equivalent of "Take it or leave it!" No. That's offensive. Instead, I say to you, "You deserve what you're asking for. It's reasonable However, this is all I can offer you in that particular pay grade: between $28,000 and $30,000. What do you want?"

Obviously, you reply, "I'll take $30,000."

I protest slightly, as though you're getting the edge in the situation: "Could you make that $29,000?"

You say, "No . . . I want $30,000."

I sigh, then capitulate. "Oh, all right. If you feel that strongly, I'll go along with it. $30,000 it is."

The same limited-menu technique works even in highly dramatic situations. In August of 1977 Croatians skyjacked a TWA aircraft scheduled to go from New York's La Guardia Airport to Chicago-O'Hare. In a stall for time, the plane was flown a serpentine route via Montreal, Newfoundland, Shannon, London, and ultimately to Charles de Gaulle Airport outside Paris, where French authorities shot out its tires.

The plane sat on the runway for three days. Finally the French police, meeting my criteria, gave the terrorists a limited-menu ultimatum, which I'll paraphrase as follows: "Look . . . you guys can do whatever you want. However, American police have arrived, and if you give up and go back to the States with them now, you'll get two to four years in prison, tops. That means you'll probably be let out in about ten months."

Waiting for a moment so that would sink in, the French continued, "But if we have to capture you, the penalty is execution, according to the law of France. Now . . . what would you like to do?"

Believe it or not, the skyjackers decided to surrender and take their chances with the American judicial system.

PART TWO

THE THREE
CRUCIAL VARIABLES

Unreality is the true source of powerlessness.
What we do not understand, we cannot control.

—Charles Reich

There is a touching moment in Arthur Miller's play *Death of a Salesman* when pathetic Willy Loman turns to his wealthy brother and asks, "Oh, Ben, how did you do it? What is the answer?"

For all of us—losers and winners alike—Willy is asking for the all-embracing formula for success in the game of life.

If life is a game, negotiation is a way of life. If you want to succeed, you must try to comprehend the game in its entirety.

Initially you must be reality oriented—seeing things as they really are without passing judgment. It is all too common for people to look at their situation selectively and pass their own moral judgment. Avoid this subjectivity, since it can only translate itself into wishful thinking. Rather, "See it like it is!" Although the subject matter and the players change from one negotiation to another, the essential ingredients are three, and they remain the same.

Picture this in your mind's eye: Several men, with faces as impassive as they can make them, huddled around a table in a smoke-filled room. It's late at night. What are they doing? They're trying to resolve something by engaging in a strategic contest, a contest governed by precedent and ritual. What's the contest about? It might easily be politics, poker . . . or negotiation.

In politics, poker, and negotiation, success derives not only from holding a strong hand, but from analyzing the total situation so cards can be skillfully played. Even the slickest, best-positioned contestant makes little headway unless he takes into account hard-nosed realities affecting everyone. You see, in order to influence an outcome—in politics, poker, or negotiation—you must realistically analyze the other side's position, as well as your own, in light of three ever-present tightly interrelated variables:

1. POWER
2. TIME
3. INFORMATION

If you think you can or you can't,
you're always right.

—Henry Ford I

4. Power

Earlier, I defined power as the capacity or ability to get things done . . . to exercise control over people, events, situations, oneself. As such, it isn't good or bad. It isn't moral or immoral. It isn't ethical or unethical. It's neutral.

Power is a way of getting from one place to another. Let's say you're currently at position A (your present situation or predicament). You want to go to position B (your objective, goal, or destination). Power enables you to go from A to B. It enables you to change your reality to *achieve* that goal.

"Power" is a concept with ugly connotations. Why? Because it implies a master-slave relationship, with one side dominating the other. This blanket indictment is out of touch with life's realities. When knowledgeable people complain about power, it is for one of two reasons:

1. They don't like the way it's being used. It's being employed in a manipulative, coercive, or domineering

way; power *over* rather than power *to*. Power is being abused, and the criticism is valid.

2. They don't approve of power's goal. If the desired end or destination is considered corrupt and exploitative, even the most appropriate means won't make that end acceptable.

Other than in these two instances, I see no objection to the use of power. Power should never be a goal in and of itself. It should be transport to a destination. If we split power from its many possible goals, the goals may be delightfully "good" or abominably "bad," but the power to implement the goals is a neutral force like electricity or wind. Now, you and I know that electricity isn't all bad because occasionally someone gets a shock from it. Air, in the form of wind, isn't bad simply because it occasionally twirls into tornadoes. Most of the time, air simply slides in and out of our lungs. We need it; without it, our bodies would self-destruct. We also need power to protect ourselves and to ensure that we have a sense of mastery over our lives.

You have plenty of power. Use it to sensibly implement objectives that are important to you. You owe it to yourself not to live by what someone else thinks you ought to do.

If you're aware of an injustice—to yourself or someone else—you have the power to act. If you turn away because you believe you are helpless ("What can one person do?"), you'll no doubt feel frustrated and wretched.

When people in our society believe they can't, as individuals, make a difference, it's bad for all of us. "Powerless" people become apathetic and toss in the towel, which means others have to carry them on their backs, or they become hostile and try to tear down a system they can't understand and don't believe they can control. This attitude pervades our world. Some of its symptoms are declining productivity and senseless violence.

Lynette "Squeaky" Fromme was one of those who became hostile. She attempted to gun down President Gerald Ford. After her arrest, she explained, "When people around you treat you like a child and pay no attention to the things you say, you have to do *something!*"

The "something" Squeaky did was psychopathic and self-destructive. Her self-perception was miles off base. She didn't realize that she had other alternatives that were socially acceptable and legal. She didn't realize that a criminal act, regardless of its goal, is almost always an abuse of power.

In essence, power is neutral. It's a means, not an end. It's indispensable for mental health and nonaggressive survival—and is based upon perception.

Let me illustrate what I mean when I say you have power if you *perceive* that you have it. Imagine a prisoner in solitary confinement. The authorities have removed his shoe laces and his belt, because they don't want him to hurt himself. (They are saving him for them for later on.) The wretch slouches back and forth in his cell, holding up his pants with his left hand, not only because he's minus a belt, but because he's minus fifteen pounds. The food they shove under the steel door is slop, and he refuses to eat it. But now, as he runs his fingertips over his ribs, his nostrils pick up the scent of a Marlboro cigarette, his favorite brand.

Through a tiny porthole in the door, he watches as the lone guard in the corridor sucks in a lungful, then exhales blissfully. Desperate for a cigarette, the prisoner respectfully taps on the door with the knuckles of his right hand.

The guard ambles over and contemptuously grunts, "Whaddya want?"

The prisoner replies, "I'd like a cigarette, please . . . the kind you're smoking: a Marlboro."

The guard mistakenly perceives the prisoner as powerless, so he snorts derisively and turns his back.

The prisoner perceives his situation differently. He's aware of his options; he's willing to test his assumptions and take risks. So he taps again on the door with the knuckles of his right hand, this time commandingly.

The guard, exhaling a cloud of smoke, irritatedly turns his head. "Now whatddya want?"

The prisoner responds, "Please, I would like one of your cigarettes within the next thirty seconds. If I don't get it, I'm going to bang my head against the concrete wall till I'm a bloody mess and unconscious. When the prison officials pick me off the floor and revive me, I'll swear *you* did it.

"Now, they'll never believe me, but think of all the hearings you'll have to attend and the commissions you'll be testifying before. Think of the reports you'll have to fill out in triplicate. Think of the administrivia you'll be tangled in—*all that as opposed to giving me one crummy Marlboro!* Just one cigarette, and I promise not to bother you again."

Does the guard slip him a cigarette through the tiny porthole? Yes. Does he light it for him? Yes. Why? Because the guard has done a fast cost-benefit analysis of the situation.

Whatever your circumstances, chances are that you're in a better position than that prisoner tugging up his pants with his left hand. He wanted a Marlboro, and he got it. *Within reason, you can get whatever you want if you're aware of your options, if you test your assumptions, if you take shrewdly calculated risks based on solid information, and if you believe you have power.*

The formula is almost laughably simple. Believe firmly that you have power, and you'll convey that self-confident perception to others. It is you who determine how they see, believe, and react to you.

Succinctly stated, power is their perception that you can, and just might, bring about intended effects that they believe might help them or hurt them. Although power, like beauty, is strictly in the eye of the beholder . . . it begins with you!

Speaking of power being in the eye of the beholder, remember the motion picture *The Wizard of Oz*? There's an individual who exercises a lot of power in that film: the Great, Mighty, Powerful Wizard. He has Dorothy and her friends spending much of their time doing very dangerous things as they attempt to steal the broomstick belonging to the Wicked Witch of the West. They obediently risk their lives in pursuit of this goal because they think the Wizard has power.

At the end of the film, when Toto, the dog, yanks the curtain back, who does the Wizard turn out to be? Just a bumbling old codger with a smoke machine and a noisemaker. In reality the old geezer had no power, but he exercised a great deal of power because everyone was convinced he had it. Up to the unmasking, everyone else's perception was based on the Wizard's self-perception.

Unlike the Wizard, you needn't fake your power. *You have more power sources at your fingertips than you realize!*

1. The power of competition

Whenever you create competition for something you possess —in the Sears example, money—what you have moves up in value. Obviously, the more people who want your money, the further your money will go.

This applies not only to products or services, if you're a seller—and to money, if you're a consumer—but also to something as abstract as an idea. Suppose I'm your immediate supervisor at work, and you rush into my office and say, "Herb! I have a marvelous idea . . . a new concept that's really something!" If I then ask you, "Have you discussed it with anyone else?" and you reply, "Yes, a number of other supervisors, but they don't think it's worth very much," does that enhance the value of your idea in my eyes? No. Your idea is devalued because there's no competition for it.

But if in response to my question you reply, "Yes . . . I talked it over with others at your level, and they said they'd like to hear more, because it sounds terrific!" my reaction will be, "Close the door, sit down, and tell me all about it!"

because through creating competition, you've made your idea valuable and desirable.

Continuing with the power of competition, is it easier to get a job when you already have one or when you don't? Of course, the answer is that it's easier to get a job when you already have one.

Consider this scenario: You apply for a position. For some reason, you've been unemployed for twelve months. I examine your qualifications and then politely ask, "What have you done, in the past year, to keep yourself challenged?"

You clear your throat and say, "Not very much." You tell me you've been a domestic engineer . . . or a consultant.

I reply, "Thanks—I'll get back to you."

Your anxiety now causes you to lose your cool. You blurt, "But, when? Could you give me a date?"

I detect that you're under stress because you lack options. I'm thinking, "How good can this person be, if no one else wants him?" I smile woodenly and answer your query with: "Our office will correspond with you in the near future."

You lick your lower lip and whisper, "But when?"

I try to make my smile less wooden as I think, "What difference does it make? You aren't going anywhere!"

Cross-fade to another scenario. You need a loan. You're concerned because, as an "average person" in today's economy, you know that you aren't the only one short of cash.

Have banks pounded on your door, offering you their services? No.

Finally, after much footdragging, you whip up enough courage to enter the local financial institution. Is it a good policy to hesitatingly approach the bank's lending officer on bended knee and say, in effect, "Please help me. I'm destitute. Save my family from the horrors of bankruptcy. I have no collateral, and probably can't repay what you lend me, but you'll be rewarded in the next world for your generosity"? That is *not* an approach that works.

Here's the approach to use: If you're a man, put on a

gray, three-piece bank-loan suit. If you're a woman, put on a conservative-looking dress suit. Wear an expensive gold watch and a Phi Beta Kappa key if you can borrow one. Have three of your friends—your entourage—outfit themselves the same way. Walk through the bank, exuding vibrations that say, "Hi there! I'm a top executive striding through the bank. Keep away from me with your lousy money . . . I don't need it. I'm on my way to mail a letter!" Do that, and the lending officer will follow you out of the bank and breathlessly trail you halfway home.

Incidentally, what I've just described is what I call The Bert Lance Theory of Money Acquisition. Remember Lance? He served as President Jimmy Carter's federal budget director. By using the "Keep away from me with your lousy money" ploy, he was granted 381 loans by 41 banks: loans totaling more than twenty million dollars. *Twenty million dollars!* Why did banks compete with each other to lend huge sums of money to Lance? For three reasons:

1. Because other banks were lending him money, which for all practical purposes meant his credit was first-rate.
2. Because banks thought he didn't need the money. That was their perception, based on the fact that he acted blasé. He seemingly hadn't a care in the world. Lance's attitude was that he was doing banks a favor by giving them the *opportunity* to lend him money.
3. Most important, because he obviously had options—which he milked for all they were worth. His options were that he could borrow from any bank he wanted to, picking and choosing as he saw fit. This put banks in dog-eat-dog competition with each other to push money into his hands.

When the same banks learned that Lance desperately needed these loans to pay back other loans, his sources dried up.

My point is that Bert Lance perceived that he had options and capitalized on them. He cashed in on the competition he created. You should do the same whenever possible. Above all, *never enter a negotiation without options*. If you do, the other side will treat you lightly, as in the needing-a-job and the selling-an-idea examples I just gave you.

2. The power of legitimacy

Another source of power at your disposal is the power of legitimacy.

In our society, people are conditioned to regard with awe anything printed. Printed words, documents, and signs carry authority. Most people tend not to question them.

I'm telling you, flat out, that as you negotiate your way through life, legitimacy *can* be questioned and challenged. I'm also advising you, flat out, to use the power of legitimacy when it's advantageous and to challenge that power when it's advantageous for you to do so.

What I've just said is so important, it's worth repeating: *Legitimacy can be questioned and challenged. Use the power of legitimacy when it's advantageous for you to do so and challenge that power when it's advantageous for you to do so.*

Here's an instance of *challenging* the power of legitimacy: Three years ago, the Internal Revenue Service called me in to audit my tax return. I had purchased a building, which I had depreciated over a number of years when filing my taxes. During a review of my return an IRS auditor claimed, for the record, that the building should be depreciated over thirty years. I said, for the record, that it should be depreciated over twenty. Why did I take that position? Well, that's what I had on my income-tax return, and I thought it would be a good idea to be consistent during the audit.

The auditor muttered, "Thirty-year depreciation!"

I muttered, "Twenty-year depreciation!"

With a scowl on his face, he reached into his bottom desk

drawer, yanked out a book, then thumbed through its pages. "Look," he grunted, "the book says it right here: thirty years!"

I stood up, walked to the rear of the desk, studied the page, and innocently asked, "Does that book mention my name? Does it indicate the location and address of my building?"

He replied, "Of course not!"

I countered, "Then I don't think it's my book."

To emphasize my position, I pulled other books off a shelf behind him.

He protested, "What are you *doing?*"

I replied, "I'm looking for *my* book—the book with my name and my building in it."

The auditor said, "Come on, put those back on the shelf. You can't argue with the book!"

"Why not?" I asked.

He made a face. "Because no one ever did it before!"

I smiled, "Well . . . let me be the first!"

Think about the book I successfully challenged. Was it a statute enacted by Congress? No. Was it a decree from on high? No. It was an IRS document, which was the product of a negotiation, drawn up by bureaucrats to interpret a regulation that was also the product of a negotiation. Since the book's position was the end result of a negotiation, the matter was negotiable.

Here's an instance of *using* the power of legitimacy. Allen Funt's *Candid Camera* has been a popular TV show for decades. The show is based on the incredible effect legitimacy has on most people, regardless of sex, education, or background. In one episode, aired several years ago, Funt closed down the state of Delaware for an hour and a half. How? By positioning a large sign over a major expressway—a sign that simply stated:

DELAWARE CLOSED

Lines of cars squealed to a halt. Vehicles pulled off the highway. Confused drivers stepped out and approached Funt, who stood beneath the sign as hidden movie cameras recorded the event. Scores blurted variations of "Hey! What's the story on Delaware?"

Funt merely pointed overhead and replied, "Read the sign!"

The drivers frowned, scratched their heads, then tugged their lower lips. One asked: "When do you think it'll reopen? I live there, and my family is in there."

Obviously, legitimacy is extremely potent in our society. Tap in on its power. Use your head and tap in on the power of risk taking as well.

3. The power of risk taking

You must be willing to take risks while negotiating. Risk taking involves mixing courage with common sense. If you don't take calculated chances, the other side will manipulate you. As Flip Wilson said, "Before you can hit the jackpot, you have to put a coin in the machine."

A man named Smith approached me during a break in one of my recent seminars and said, "Herb, I'm glad I came to this session. I have a problem. My family and I are in the process of moving, and we've found a house we're crazy about. We call it our dream house."

I looked at him and said, "So?"

He continued, "So . . . the seller wants $150,000 and I'm only prepared to pay $130,000. How can I get this house for $130,000, though the seller wants $20,000 more? Give me some negotiation tactics."

I asked, "What would happen if you didn't get this dream house?"

He replied, "Are you kidding? I think my wife would kill herself! I think my kids would leave home!"

I then murmured, "H-m-m-m. Tell me . . . how do you feel about your wife and kids?"

His answer was, "Come on, Herb . . . I love them very

much! I'll do anything for them! We just *have* to bring the asking price down."

Take a guess. Did Smith pay $130,000 for the dream house or $150,000? You're right, he paid $150,000. With his attitude he's lucky he didn't pay $160,000. That house meant so much to him that he was unwilling to risk losing it. Because he cared too much (moral: Care, but never *that* much), he couldn't afford any uncertainty ("Maybe there's another house I could get interested in . . ."), uncertainty that might have caused the seller to adjust the asking price downward. He held on to the electric live wire, so to speak, and couldn't let go, because he had nothing else to grab. The result was that he paid through the nose. Remember: When you feel you *have* to have something, you always pay top dollar. You put yourself in a position where the other party can manipulate you with ease.

Intelligent risk taking involves a knowledge of the "odds," plus a philosophical willingness to shrug your shoulders and absorb a manageable loss without whining ("That's the way the ball bounces"). Obviously, the chance of a setback is the price you must pay for any progress.

When I say you should be willing to take risks, I'm not advocating that you do anything as idiotic as risking your savings account on the spin of a Las Vegas roulette wheel. I'm not proposing that you take far-out chances that might tempt you to slash your wrists if the wheel of fortune stops at the wrong number. I *am* suggesting that you take moderate or incremental risks: risks you can afford without being uptight about adverse consequences.

Let me give you an example about calculating the odds, followed by a suggestion on how you can make your risks more manageable. At a particular point in one of my negotiating seminars, I stand before the group with an ordinary quarter in my hand and say, "I'm about to do the traditional coin flip. I'll flip this twenty-five-cent piece just once. If you call heads or tails correctly, I'll give you a million dollars. If you call heads or tails incorrectly you have to give me a hundred thousand dollars. Assuming that this is a legitimate bet and that I'm not kidding around . . . how many of you in this room would *take* this bet?"

Normally, no one raises a hand. I flip the coin, glance at it, and slide it back into my pocket. Then I comment, "Let me try to analyze what went through your minds when I made this proposition. You said to yourselves, 'This guy is giving me ten-to-one odds on a fifty-fifty bet. He may know a lot about negotiation, but statistically, he isn't very bright!' "

Most of the audience nods in agreement. I keep talking: "Were you thinking of winning? Were you trying to figure out what you'd do with a million dollars? Perhaps work out a tax shelter, then head for Tahiti? No. You were thinking of losing. You were thinking, 'How can I possibly scrounge up a hundred thousand bucks? Right now I'm a little short until payday!' "

Many members of the audience laugh nervously. I continue, "I can imagine some of you walking into your home after the seminar. Your spouse greets you and says, 'Did anything unusual happen?' You reply, 'Well, there was this guy, and he had a quarter, and he did this coin flip. By the way, how liquid are we right now? Is there any cash lying around?' "

The audience is wise in not taking me up on that coin flip. The degree of risk to anyone, in such a monetary situation, is proportional to what that person already has in the way of assets. If anyone in the audience were a multimillionaire, he or she might challenge me on the gamble. J. Paul Getty or Howard Hughes wouldn't have given it a second thought. The old saying is still valid: "Money goes to money."

Possession of wealth enables one to explore favorable opportunities, for the inherent risk is moderate. It's no more than bite-size. In case of loss, the wealthy person can shrug and exclaim, "How *about* that!"

Supposing I quantitatively reduced the bet's equation?

Supposing I switched from a million dollars versus a hundred thousand dollars to a more manageable hundred dollars versus ten? Would anyone in the audience take me up on the bet? The chances are that almost everyone present would, since the risk is now no more than incremental with respect to their assets.

Keep in mind that the ratio between the two figures is still the same, but the possibility of a crippling loss has been eliminated. Most of us can handle the potential loss of ten dollars without flinching. Few can absorb the possible loss of a hundred thousand dollars without chewing the wallpaper.

Even if I don't reduce the bet's equation, the audience can make the risk manageable if they *syndicate* it or spread it out. Here's what I mean by that: If each of the thousand people in the audience drops a hundred dollars in a kitty, and a chosen representative calls the coin flip correctly, one million dollars will be split equally among one thousand individuals. This moves the equation into an entirely new light, for the fifty-fifty possibility of losing involves only one hundred dollars, which is fairly unpleasant but not disastrous. However— and here's the clincher—the fifty-fifty possibility of winning involves one-thousandth of a million dollars, or a whopping one thousand dollars.

So when much is at stake, always consider sharing or syndicating the risk involved. When you spread a risk so that it's on others' shoulders as well as your own, you defuse and diffuse that risk. In distributing or syndicating risks, you put yourself in the enviable position of being able to cash in on opportunities where the odds are in your favor.

By getting others involved, you also expand your horizons and increase your "staying power." Whether playing poker or investing in the stock market, you're in a stronger power position if your capital is considerably larger than your opponents'.

In encouraging you to take risks, I want you to take optimum or moderate risks. I don't want you to gamble or "shoot craps with destiny." Before chancing anything, calculate the odds to determine whether the potential benefits are worth the possible cost of failure. Be rational, not impulsive. Never take a risk out of pride, impatience, or a desire to get it over with.

4. The power of commitment

As I've just shown, getting the commitment of a large number of people when I flip the coin enables you to spread your risk among the whole group. It lets you cash in on the favorable odds. By syndicating your risk you put yourself in a position to exploit the favorable opportunity because the risk is only moderate for you. This technique of involving others should be applied to all of life's substantial endeavors where the outcome is uncertain.

For example, if you are about to embark upon a monumental, risky venture, you don't stride up to your boss, family, or associates and proclaim, "This is a big one! It's *my* idea! *My* proposal! If anything goes wrong I'll go down with it!" No. That's crazy. Rather, you walk around your office, shop, or home and remind everyone, "We're all in this together!"

In short, don't crawl out alone on a limb that might be sawed off, to become either a hero today or a zero tomorrow. Persuade others to help, get them involved in the planning and decision making, and they will shoulder part of the burden. Remember, people support that which they help create.

You can make the application of the power of commitment of others work for you in three ways:

1. By dispersing the overall risk, you can take advantage of propitious circumstances.
2. Since your associates share the total anxiety and lend their support, your stress level is reduced.
3. The shoulder-to-shoulder dedication of your group transmits awesome power vibrations to the other side.

You see, your ability to gain the commitment of others magnifies the impact of your words and gives you power. Conversely, when the other side perceives that your team or group is "singing from different hymn books," your position is undermined as in the Sears refrigerator situation, when you, your spouse, and your offspring transmitted conflicting signals to the salesman.

As a further illustration, let's assume that you and four others representing your company are about to negotiate with some people from another organization. As you approach the conference table, you assume that everyone on your team sees things your way. When the meeting starts, someone on your side makes an unexpected concession that the other side agrees with.

This generous or revealing comment from out of the blue undermines your negotiating position. Shocked, you half-believe that the other side has planted a spy in your midst. You're so upset that at the first coffee break, you testily mutter to the offender, "Are you sure you're with *our* company? Let me see your ID, so I will know whom you work for!"

What happened here was that you failed to negotiate for the commitment of every team member before entering the meeting. Moral: *Always* get the commitment of others in any undertaking. Have them take a piece of the action so it's their action as well as yours. Involvement begets commitment. Commitment begets power.

On a broader scale, you know that when a community fails to support local police, law enforcement suffers. Banks fail if confidence in their stability wanes. Armies are useless unless soldiers believe in what they're fighting for. Vietnam was lost, not because the "best and brightest" realized their mistakes, but because commitment eroded in the jungles and at home, and national policy followed. In reality, President Richard Nixon's troop withdrawal ratified a decision that had already been made by the majority who were committed to ending the war.

Returning to the fact that you need never fake your power capacity, because you have much more potential than you think, let me show you some additional sources.

5. The power of expertise

Have you ever noticed that when others perceive—or believe—that you have more technical knowledge, specialized skill, or experience than they have, they treat you with a consideration that ranges from respect to awe? I'll give you a real example and two hypothetical ones.

The real example: During World War II, General George S. Patton commanded the first Allied invasion of north Africa. Patton was one of the most egotistical men of all time. He thought he knew everything about *everything*, from poetry to ballistics. Yet he humbly accepted every word of advice given by his flagship's navigator. Why? Because the navigator had expertise that Patton admittedly lacked.

The first hypothetical example: You're redecorating your house, apartment, or condominium. You have certain wallpaper in mind, but you aren't sure it'll blend with your furniture. You hire an expensive interior decorator to dispense advice. Her work has appeared in an exclusive magazine. She tells you to use entirely different wallpaper because your selection is passé. You do so without hesitation. Why? Because for the sizable fee she charges, you assume she has savvy and expert taste that you don't have.

The second hypothetical example: You experience sharp pains in your abdomen. Your local physician refers you to a specialist in internal medicine. After giving your case history to a nurse you recall that these symptoms are similar to those you had when your gall bladder acted up three years ago. After the requisite tests and brief examination you are ushered into a room lined with certificates and diplomas (you counted fourteen while waiting). The internist arrives and issues the diagnosis: diverticulitis.

A mimeographed sheet is given to you, and you are asked, "Do you have any questions?" You respond in the negative, and the next thing you realize, you're scheduling another appointment with the receptionist. Although you can't pronounce or spell your illness, you know "you got it." Why? Who could possibly question the diagnostic proclamation in view of the physical surroundings and professional credentials of the expert?

Let me explain how you can use this attitude of acceptance, respect, and awe—which stems, in part, from the aura of mystery and magic that surrounded primitive witch doctors—in negotiating situations. You can tap in on the power of expertise because the same reverence for specialized knowledge is rampant today.

As you know, most of us rarely question the statements of tax accountants, physicians, auto mechanics, attorneys, computer specialists, stock brokers, research scientists, professors, Pentagon generals, or plumbers. Why don't we question them? Because we're somehow convinced they know more than we do about their specialties.

Here's what to do if you want to present *yourself* as having expertise: Establish your background and credentials early in the confrontation. If you do, your statements may not even be challenged. In other words, cash in on the fact that in complicated negotiations, participants often lack specialized knowledge of certain aspects of the matter being discussed.

Whenever possible, actually *have* the savvy others assume you have. Prepare yourself ahead of time. If the negotiation is important enough to you to win, it ought to be worth some of your time in boning up. (Bone up on subjects before you confer on them.) If you don't have the savvy, don't push your luck. Just make some incisive remarks, or drop a few choice words in the jargon of the experts, then keep your mouth shut.

Above all, don't be pretentious. In today's world, where "knowledge keeps about as well as dead fish" (and even under refrigeration that's not long), it's impossible to be an expert in all areas. In general the only kind of expertise required for most negotiations is the ability to ask intelligent questions and know whether you are getting accurate responses.

What if you feel you are in over your head because the other side has an expert who wrote two papers and a monograph on the subject being discussed? No problem. Use your resources (community, friends, organization, etc.) and bring in your own expert who wrote *three* papers, two monographs, and a book on the subject. Obviously, that will more than neutralize the other side.

When you are confronted by "The Expert" on the other side of the desk or table, don't be overimpressed. Keep in mind that if they didn't need you or what you have to offer, they wouldn't be there. Train yourself to occasionally say, "I don't understand. You lost me three minutes ago." Or "Can you explain that in layman's language?" A dose of irreverence, plus a dash of innocence, when combined with polite persistence and the asking of questions, will often change the attitude and behavior of the so-called expert.

6. The power of the knowledge of "needs"

In all negotiations, there are two things being bargained for:

1. The specific issues and demands, which are stated openly.
2. The *real needs* of the other side, which are rarely verbalized.

Let me illustrate this distinction by returning to the Sears refrigerator analogy. Let's assume you walk into the Large Appliances Department and say to a salesman, "Look . . . if you sell me this $489.50 model for $450, I'll pay you in cash right now!"

Will this approach work with Sears? No. The proposition

fails to meet that organization's true needs. Why? As you know, Sears may not really be a retail establishment. It merely fronts as one. Actually, Sears is a financial institution that may prefer that you charge your purchase. Why? So it can get a hefty 18 percent interest on money still to be paid on your revolving charge account.

Will this money-on-the-barrelhead approach work elsewhere? Yes; depending on where you try it. If you make the same offer to a neighborhood hardware store that is experiencing a cash-flow problem, the proprietor will probably knock you over in his haste to accept. You see, he'll be able to wheel and deal with the cash. Moreover, who can say whether he'll actually declare it on his income-tax return?

Everyone's needs are different. Sears doesn't need your cash; a small proprietor often does. *If you can establish a reasonable guess about what someone's needs are, you can predict, with remarkable certainty, what will happen in any interaction.*

Never forget that behind every apparently ruthless or uncaring organization or institution, there are ordinary people desperately striving to meet their unique needs. To successfully interact with any individual in any setup, all you have to do is determine his or her needs, then fulfill them. So when someone says to you in a negotiation, "This is my rock-bottom figure!" (Ever notice how they all use that geological semanticism?), is that their real rock bottom or their *really* real rock bottom?

Essentially what people say they want (their demands) may not be what will actually satisfy their needs. For example, let's say I intend to buy a new car. I have a particular model and a particular dealership in mind. My approach is two pronged:

1. I gather as much specific data as I can about the car itself. This isn't hard to come by. I check the *Blue Book* and *Consumer Reports*. I talk to recent buyers

of the model. I question service station mechanics who've worked on it. I jot down notes on performance, costs, and potential service problems.

2. Next, I find out as much as possible about the dealership. This information isn't hard to come by either if I ask the right people—those who've dealt with the dealer—the right questions. I pinpoint his reputation. I learn the current status of his business, the extent of the inventory he must finance, his itemized costs, and how his salespeople are compensated. I check with other competing dealerships to determine their pricing

Then, with respect to the dealer himself, I acquaint myself with his likes, dislikes, prejudices, and value system. I find out if he's the type who makes quick decisions or deliberate decisions. I discover whether he likes to take risks or whether he's an advocate of the one-in-the-hand-is-worth-two-in-the-bush outlook.

If this sounds unrealistic for you to tackle, keep in mind that you are about to invest thousands of dollars in a car that at best you hope will give you reasonably good service for some years. As I said before, if the deal is worth your time and money, it's worth preparing yourself to make it a good deal.

When face to face with the dealer, or one of his key salesmen, I probe, observe, ask questions, and listen more than I talk. This gives me valuable information that enables me to best structure the negotiation. I then adapt my purchasing style to *satisfy the real needs* of the seller. His real needs may be to bargain, to haggle like a rug merchant in an oriental bazaar. He may get a kick out of bargaining, out of matching wits. I adroitly play the game because I, too, like to negotiate over big-ticket items. I most assuredly won't meet the seller's price demands, but I'll meet his real, nonverbalized needs.

The transaction will be concluded to the satisfaction of all concerned.

7. The power of investment

We've already discussed the importance of getting the other person to invest time, money, or energy in a situation. It's the key factor in making an ultimatum work. It forms the basis of the "nibble" ("What kind of tie will you be throwing in free?"). It was crucial in the example of the three Japanese gentlemen versus the sophisticated American corporation ("Can you do it again?"). That's why, at the beginning of each encounter, you should approach people collaboratively. If you want to become competitive later, or give an ultimatum, you can . . . but only at the end, after the other side has made an investment.

There's a direct ratio between the extent of an investment and the willingness to compromise. Why was it so hard for the United States to pull out of the Vietnam War? Because by the time we tried to extricate ourselves, we had already sacrificed forty-five thousand American lives in that endeavor. We in America don't casually walk away from such a human investment.

If you buy two stocks or make two real estate investments, and one goes up in value and the other goes down, which one will you sell first? Naturally, the one that goes up. How about the other? You hang on to it for a time. You might even buy more of it because, if it was priced right before, it's certainly a bargain now. Recognize this principle of human nature. Make it work for you, not against you.

Here's another insight regarding this power: Let's say my boss commissions me to negotiate with someone named Copperfield. He states, "I want you to get this price. You can compromise on other 'throwaway' items, but not the price. The price is encased in concrete."

I start negotiating with Copperfield. We begin at theoretical square number one. I state my position; Copperfield states his. We experience difficulty but resolve our differences. We move to theoretical square two, the square having to do with price. Again I state my position; Copperfield states his. We strive to reach an agreement but can't.

I say, "Copperfield, we can return to this later."

He says, "Okay."

In other words, after much travail and irritation, we move off this issue, which was heading for an impasse.

We advance to square number three. Though it takes time, we come to terms regarding square number three's subject matter. We progress to square number four. We struggle but finally work it out. Item number five is up next, and after discussion, I finally agree to buy Copperfield's creative suggestion.

Finally, we approach the finish line, with agreement on four of the five items under discussion. Copperfield grins. He can smell the roses. The negotiation is virtually in his pocket, or so he thinks. I say, "Copperfield, can we go back to square number two?"

He says, "Certainly. Maybe we can compromise on the price."

I say, "Gee, Copperfield, I'm sorry, but there can be no compromise whatever on that issue. The price is inflexible. I need the whole thing."

Now consider where Copperfield is. If he breaks off with me at this point, he loses his entire time-and-effort investment. He has to begin again with someone else. For all he knows, the "someone else" may be far more difficult to deal with than I. Because of this, he tends to become malleable. I'll get my price.

My point is this: If you have something difficult to negotiate—an emotional issue, or a concrete item that can be stated numerically, such as price, cost, interest rate, or salary—*cope with it at the end of a negotiation, after the other side has made a hefty expenditure of energy and a substantial time investment.*

What if the emotional issue or quantifiable item surfaces at the beginning of the negotiation? Acknowledge it, chat about it, but put it off till later—returning to it only after the other side has spent a lot of time with you. You'll be surprised how the other side's investment will cause them to become flexible at the end of the negotiation.

8. The power of rewarding or punishing

Your perception that I can and might help you or hurt you —physically, financially, or psychologically—gives me "muscle" in our relationship. The "actual, factual" reality of the situation is immaterial. If you *think* I can and might do something to affect you (even though I can't or won't), I will exercise power in my dealings with you. It's this perception, true or false, that gives the boss's secretary massive clout, as it did yesteryear's king's mistress. (It's the shortsighted salesman who treats the boss's secretary as if she's an insignificant member of the team. The smart person knows she can often smooth his way or scatter broken glass in his path.)

Since all people are unique, what's perceived as threatening by one is considered harmless by another. What someone perceives as a reward, someone else regards as no big deal. Rewards and coercions . . . positive and negative strokes . . . come in as many forms as there are individual perceptions and needs. *If I'm aware of your perceptions and needs, and if I know you think I have power over you, I can control your behavior.*

Supposing you think I can call the shots regarding whether you get a promotion or raise, whether you get fired, when you go to lunch, whether you get reprimanded in front of others, where your desk or office is situated, whether you get a company car, whether you have a private parking slot, when your vacation is scheduled, or whether your budget or expense account is increased. If these matters are important to you, does that make you treat me with kid gloves? You'd better believe it.

Descending to the seemingly trivial: Supposing I know you feel it's crucial that I pause at your desk and say good morning every day or send you a Christmas or birthday card. Can I make you curry my favor by neglecting to say good morning or by failing to send you a card? Again, you'd better believe it.

If some of this seems to be small potatoes—as insignificant as a glass of warm milk to a dedicated wino—that's the way it is in the real world. I'm not saying you should take advantage of this perceived power if others think you have it. I'm just saying you must be aware of the reality of the situation.

Here are two things to remember:

1. No one will ever negotiate with you in any significant way unless they're convinced that you can and might help them—or can and might hurt them.

2. In an adversary relationship, if you think I might help you or hurt you, I should never defuse your perception of my power unless I get something in return, such as a concession on your part, or a repositioning on your part, that truly benefits me or our relationship.

And here's what I mean by not defusing the perception of power (whether the perception is true or false). When President Jimmy Carter first came into office, he talked about human rights in foreign policy. There was nothing wrong with that. Unfortunately, he immediately spelled out what we would or wouldn't do. In the eyes of some adversaries this promptly transformed us into a paper tiger, no more threatening than your neighbor's kitten. He made the unfortunate mistake of publicly eliminating options without getting something in return.

For instance, as the world's moral leader, President Carter

announced that the United States would never send troops to Africa or the Middle East. Fidel Castro, munching a cigar, said, in effect, "What do you know? The Americans aren't going to send armed forces into Africa! How considerate of them! In that case, Cuba *will* send armed forces into Africa!" And Cuba did, putting troops into Angola and the Horn of Africa.

The President *should* have kept Castro off-balance. He *should* have kept open the perceived option (whether used or not) of meeting aggression with diplomatic pressure or even military force. He *should* have said, "We're the moral leader, but we don't know exactly what we will or won't do. Come to think of it, aren't we the guys who sent B-52s over Hanoi on Christmas Eve? Who knows *what* our fighting men plan to do when the weather gets colder!"

If he'd said that, Castro would have let his cigar sputter out, and if Cuban mercenaries had gone to Africa they would have glanced skyward each time a plane broke through the clouds.

Moral: Don't transform yourself into a paper tiger. In a competitive situation don't eliminate options and reduce the other side's stress unless you receive quid pro quo. Let them wonder until you have received what you're shooting for. In geopolitics the perception that you are willing to take risks and exercise power may prevent opportunism by a potential aggressor.

9. The power of identification

You will maximize your negotiating ability if you get others to identify with you.

Let me explain. Why do you prefer one store to another in the same shopping center? Why do you take your car to the same service station time after time? Why do you have your checking account at one bank and not another? In the business world, why do you deal with one company and not its competitors?

It's not just because of quality, convenience, price, or cost factors. What tips the scale one way or the other is your degree of identification with the people you come in contact with or are exposed to.

If someone at Macy's makes you feel good, important, or at least comfortable and understands your needs, you'll identify with and favor Macy's, even if Bloomingdale's offers something that looks better. That's why your ability to have others identify with you is crucial, whomever you're dealing with and for whatever reason.

For example, much of the success of the IBM Corporation stems from the professionalism of their people, not just in appearance but in their approach to customers. Several years ago I asked a corporate client why they purchased an expensive system from IBM rather than from one of its competitors. My client responded, "We could have got it cheaper elsewhere, and technically the IBM quality was not the best. However, it's a complex system, and we know that if we got into trouble they would help us." Now *that's* identification!

How do you get others to identify with you? If you act as a professional and reasonable person in dealing with people you can gain their cooperation, loyalty, and respect. Don't pull rank or overplay your authority. Rather, try to convey understanding and empathy. Speak to the other person's needs, hopes, dreams, and aspirations. Approach each person on a human level with the hope that you can help them solve their problem. If you exhibit this behavior you will release a subtle, persuasive kind of power reminiscent of the magic appeal of the Pied Piper of Hamelin.

When we speak of leadership and charisma we are often talking about individuals who conduct themselves in such a respected fashion that they inspire emulation. Those who follow a leader, sometimes at great sacrifice, so identify with that person that they feel that his or her triumphs are their own!

History is replete with examples from Buddha and Christ

to General Dwight Eisenhower and Mother Teresa. Although hardly in the same class, media stars owe their popularity to the widespread identification that they engender. Johnny Carson, host of the *Tonight Show* on television, may need a trailer truck to hold his money, but he comes across on your TV screen as likable, decent, open, and honest with his feelings. His self-deprecating wit makes him human and transmits empathetic vibes into living rooms and bedrooms across North America. We like him.

The power of identification exists in all interpersonal relationships including business transactions and politics. For instance, I'm sometimes in situations where I'm exposed to several experts who take turns discussing an issue's many aspects. What I normally do—in addition to relying on my homework—is to give more credence to the statements of a person I know and respect: a person with a proven track record. I go along, when feasible, with his or her feelings and insights, because I trust and *identify* with him or her.

We rarely admit to or talk about this identification, but it's a big factor in our decisions from the stereo we purchase to the political candidate we support. Where data and facts abound and issues are complex, we are all influenced by those with whom we can identify. As a result, people may even vote against their own economic self-interest because they can identify strongly with a political candidate.

Identification also works in reverse. One person may be right on the issues but is such a bigot and so obnoxious that he or she completely turns us off. Many people vote for candidate A not because of any degree of affinity, but because they cannot stomach candidate B. This is true in all of our dealings and decision making.

Let me tell you about my own experience with this principle.

A couple of decades ago, when I got out of law school, there was a recession in America. No one told me there was a recession, so when I couldn't get a job I took it personally. Ten years later, when I learned there had been a recession at that time, I felt much better.

After a short period of unemployment I went to work for the Legal Aid Society, defending indigent people charged with petty crimes.

One of the first people I represented was a man accused of burglary. As I look back on the case I believe he was probably guilty. Why do I say that? (1) He had given two separate confessions to two different law-enforcement agencies; (2) he had left his fingerprints all over the scene of the crime; and (3) when he was apprehended he was watching the stolen television set.

This was not what you would call a strongly defensible case.

Regardless of the odds, I was young and conscientious and attempted to see that my client received his full rights under the law. In trying to establish a defense I went to visit the defendant in prison. After several interviews in which he constantly changed his story and alibi, it was evident to me that my client was stupid and a liar. I hesitated to put him on the witness stand because I knew the contradictions in his story would be easily exposed.

Since I had to put *someone* on the stand to testify for him, I selected his mother. Mothers will always testify for their children, whatever the circumstances. My client's mother was quite presentable: a gray-haired old lady with thick glasses and a cane—the type of woman one automatically helps across streets.

After she was guided to the witness chair, I started to question her. Within two minutes, it was evident that my client's problem was, in part, genetic. The mother was also stupid and a liar. She contradicted herself four times in 120 seconds. My mouth went dry, and I sat down, knowing in my heart that the case was lost.

For some strange reason the prosecutor was not willing to leave well enough alone. He confronted the elderly lady and began a sharp cross-examination. Apparently he not only wanted to find her son, the defendant, guilty, but he wanted to find the defendant *very* guilty, super guilty, one of the most guilty defendants ever tried in that court.

In attempting to discredit the mother as a witness, he practiced what we now call overkill. He baited the old lady, badgered her, shouted at her, berated her. She broke down and whimpered. Then she sobbed and as she wiped the tears from her eyes, her glasses fell from her face. Stepping back, the prosecutor accidentally crushed her spectacles under his heel.

After hastily calling a recess, the judge gestured to me to help the now hysterical old lady down from the stand. As I did so, I happened to glance at the jury. Suddenly, amazed, I knew what was about to happen. That jury loathed the prosecutor. I'm certain they were thinking, "It's bad enough that this poor mother has a son who's a criminal. Does that monster of a prosecutor have to subject her to this kind of abuse too?"

The jury returned quickly with a verdict of not guilty—one of the few victories I had at that stage of my life.

Please don't blame me for that miscarriage of justice. I didn't *win* that case. The other side *lost* the case. Why? Because the facts were so clouded over by the prosecutor's behavior that the jury couldn't identify with either him or the valid points he tried to make. The jury's vote went contrary to the evidence presented.

More often than people care to admit, identification (whether with or against) plays a significant role in negotiations and decision making. That's why behaving decently and trying to help others is the equivalent of having a canteen of water in the Gobi Desert.

10. The power of morality

Most of us raised in the Western world are imprinted with similar ethical and moral standards. We learned them from the schools or churches we attended or observed them in action in our family situations, and we picked them up from our acquaintances in the business world and on the street. Whatever, our concepts of fairness tend to be very much alike. Few of us can walk through life without believing that what we're doing is for the good of mankind—or "peoplekind."

That's why, if you lay morality on people in an unqualified way, it may often work. And if you throw yourself on their mercy without defense or pretense there's a chance they may succumb. Why? Because they can relate to you and are hesitant to take advantage of someone who is truly defenseless.

Even if someone has the law on his side and theoretically can crush you, if you say, "You can do anything you want with me . . . but would it be the right thing?" your appeal for mercy has a fighting chance. This is true even in the judicial system. Defendants sometimes throw themselves on the mercy of courts, and courts occasionally grant mercy.

For example, a defendant, standing before a judge, may plead, "Judge, would putting me behind bars for a long time be the right thing? I have three small children at home. I have a wife. By sending me away, you're only penalizing *them*. Judge, I don't mind taking my punishment, but think of what a long sentence would do to my family. Judge, I know I deserve to be sent away forever for this crime, but would it be the right thing for my innocent family?" Chances are, the judge will think long and hard about sentencing.

Will this type of appeal work with people who have different values in other cultures? No. Will it work with those whose imprinting is entirely different? No. People who are programmed in ways alien to us, such as fundamentalist Shiite Muslims, can't comprehend our concepts of forgiveness, cheek turning, and extended olive branches. What they understand is power, opportunism, and revenge. Don't be made a sucker by such people. You should deal with people based on *their* frame of reference.

However, most people you come into contact with share your background. So if someone close to you—your spouse, your boss, or a subordinate, for instance—shafts you by putting you down, letting you down, taking a cheap shot, exercising malicious obedience, or not doing what he or she promised, ask the other party if it was fair and right. Not surprisingly, that question shakes up even the most worldly, self-seeking, and jaded.

11. The power of precedent

I mentioned this power with respect to the Sears refrigerator situation, when I said that most people believe they can't negotiate with a one-price store. If I ask them why, they reply, "Why else would they call it a one-price store?"

I also said: Don't act as though your limited experience represents universal truths. Force yourself to go outside your experience by testing your assumptions. Don't lock yourself into time-worn ways of doing things.

It's easy to lock yourself in—or to get locked in by others—because one aspect of the power of precedent is based on a "Don't make waves," "You can't argue with success," and "We've always done it this way" outlook. This aspect stems from applying pressure to do things the way they're currently being done . . . or to do things the way they were done before. Current and past customs, policies, and practices are considered sacred. They're presented as the *only* way to do things. "Change" is a dirty six-letter word.

For example, one of the thorniest tasks facing a new president in Washington, a new corporation head in any business, or a new leader of any long-established organization, is changing deeply ingrained past practices. After the 1968 election, Richard Nixon proclaimed, "It's time to get big government off your back and out of your pocket!" A few weeks later he proposed the biggest federal budget in the nation's history.

But here's another aspect of the power of precedent: It can be used as an *excuse* for change. When the United Auto

Workers in the United States achieved a seven percent pay
increase in their contract, the Canadian auto workers, using
the United States example as justification, promptly negotiated for and achieved the same pay increase. The logic involved was simple: "There's our model. They got it; we should
get it too."

The mayor of Memphis, Tennessee, publicly announced
that all policemen and firemen going on strike would be fired.
They went on strike and lost their jobs. Several days later, a
settlement was reached and the mayor reinstated them. Consequently, the Chicago firefighters went on strike, with the
expectation that even if they were suspended, they were likely
to be reinstated after a settlement was reached. Subsequent
events proved them correct.

In other words, if people at point A do something and
people at point B learn about it, it affects the way people at
point B act. Information spreads fast. We're all tuned to the
same TV station. So if you're trying to control a situation
and you don't want what happens at A to influence what happens at B, be prepared to show people at B why their set-up
differs from the A set-up.

While avoiding being "taken in" by the power of precedent,
use this power to your advantage. To justify what you're
doing or asking for, always refer to other situations similar
to the one you're currently in, where you or others did so-and-
so, and the result you wanted occurred.

For instance, if you're at a retail outlet, trying to negotiate the price of an item so it's less of a drain on your wallet,
and the salesperson says, "I'm sorry—you know we don't negotiate!" what do you do? You say, "Wait a minute—of
course you do! I bought a hammer here, in your hardware
section, just two weeks ago. It was chipped, and the clerk
gave me two dollars off!"

Use the binding "logic" of popular tradition, though the
tradition actually may be illogical. If you're buying an appliance or a car, say, "I want *last* year's model, not this year's."

Why do you say this? Because everyone knows that last year's model is cheaper than this year's, even though last year's model may be in mint condition. Do you know the difference between a 1980 and a 1981 refrigerator model? Perhaps one has tail fins. In dollars-and-cents terms, the concept doesn't hold water if the model or appliance hasn't been used, but folklore and precedent are heavily in your favor. Cash in on them.

12. The power of persistence

Persistence is to power what carbon is to steel. By gnawing through a dike long enough even a rat can drown a nation.

Most people aren't persistent enough when negotiating. They present something to the other side, and if the other side doesn't "buy" it right away, they shrug and move on to something else. If that's a quality you have, I suggest you change it. Learn to hang in there. You must be tenacious. That's an admirable quality President Carter has. He's tenacious. He's steadfast. He's remarkably persistent.

In my opinion, President Carter is an extremely moral, decent, ethical person. However, at the same time, he may be one of the most boring leaders in American history. When you spend more than fifteen minutes with him it's like taking a sedative. Someone once commented, "When Carter gives a Fireside Chat, the fire usually goes out." In short, if he enters a room, it's as though someone had just left.

But he effectively used his reverse charisma on Anwar Sadat of Egypt and Menachem Begin of Israel at his secluded presidential retreat in the Maryland hills.

Camp David is *not* the Sodom and Gomorrah of the Western world. It's emphatically *not* a place for swingers—even for the moderately alive. The most exciting activity there is sniffing pine cones.

Knowing this, and realizing he wanted to achieve "acceptable minimum results," Carter cleverly saw to it that there were only two bicycles for fourteen people and a total lack of other recreational facilities. Evenings, to relax, those present for the extended stay had a choice of watching one of three insipid motion pictures. By the sixth day, everyone had seen the films twice and they were bored out of their minds.

But every day at 8:00 A.M. Sadat and Begin heard the usual knock on their cabin door followed by the same familiar monotone, "Hi, it's Jimmy Carter, ready for another ten boring hours of the same dull stuff." By the thirteenth day of this, if you were Sadat and Begin, you would have signed *anything* to get out of there. The Camp David peace agreement was a classic, attributable to the patience and persistence of Jimmy Carter.

You aren't personally involved in Camp David peace agreements, but you *are* personally involved in many other situations. Let's say you've locked horns with your insurance company over a claim. Your six-year-old car, which was in excellent condition, was totaled in an accident. Its book value is listed as only $500. Yet you can't replace that car for less than $800. You don't *care* what the book says. The book is nothing but a collection of black marks on white paper anyway.

What should you do?

You should emphatically convey to the insurance company that you'll settle for nothing less than $800. You do this by saying, "I'm perfectly willing to go to court . . . with all the attendant costs and publicity!"

Will your comment about attendant costs and publicity prick up the claims adjuster's ears? You can bet a bottle of your favorite bourbon on it. He knows that litigation means delay, uncertainty, inquiries from government agencies and the state Department of Insurance, plus a damaged reputation for his company in its dealings with claimants. He also knows that a lawsuit entails legal costs and the setting aside of reserves that might otherwise be invested profitably.

There also may be practical considerations that discourage the insurance company from facing you in court . . . considerations that can range from the unavailability of witnesses to the backbreaking workload of their counsel.

Will you get your $800? Yes—if you keep talking to the adjuster and his superiors, write letters, and furnish additional information (repair bills and receipts) that justify your claim that this auto was a "unique vehicle" not within the purview of the book. Persistence pays off.

13. The power of persuasive capacity

Most of us, in our civilized society, rely too heavily on reasoning capacity to make things happen. We've been raised to believe that logic will prevail. Logic, in and of itself, will rarely influence people. Most often logic doesn't work.

If you want to persuade me to believe something, do something, or buy something, you must rely on three factors:

1. I have to understand what you're saying. It's imperative that you put your reasons into analogies that relate to my experiences, my particular imprinting. In order to do this, you must enter my world. (That's why it's so hard for you to negotiate with someone who's stupid or who you think is a lunatic.)
2. Your evidence must be so overwhelming that I can't dispute it.
3. My believing you must meet my existing needs and desires.

Of these three factors, the third (meeting my needs and desires) is, by far, the most important. Why do I say that? Because even if you present me with overwhelming evidence that I understand, should the conclusion depress me, I will remain unconvinced. Your facts and logic may be unassailable, but their acceptance will not meet my existing needs and desires. Parents of teenage children understand this illogical phenomenon better than most, but it's the basis of much failure in persuasion.

The advertising industry, whose business it is to motivate behavior, uses this concept to influence prospective consumers. You've all seen a certain deodorant commercial on television. You put one spray—psst . . . psst—under each arm, and for twenty-four hours a day, an invisible shield forms around your body. The advertiser couldn't care less whether you or I understand the commercial, or whether there is evidence to support his claim. The advertiser simply wants to demonstrate how this spray meets *your* needs and desires to be socially acceptable.

I'll be honest with you: *I* don't understand that commercial. I know there's no evidence to support the invisible-shield theory. I've never seen an invisible shield, nor do I know anyone who has, and not only because it's invisible! But I like *believing* in an invisible shield that surrounds me. Believing in the shield makes me feel at ease and confident in any situation.

Let's say that we meet on a social occasion and that I lean forward to tell you something privately. You pull back slightly. Had I not sprayed two hours earlier, I might regard your movement as a cue that I have a personal-hygiene problem. But since I have at least twenty more hours of the invisible shield enveloping me, I figure that the person beside you, whom you came with, is in trouble.

Speaking of problems, for centuries everyone thought the sun revolved around the earth. People knew in their bones that the earth was the center of the universe. Along came a brilliant man named Copernicus, who tried to upset *that* applecart by propounding a new theory about the solar system. He stated, flat out, that the earth revolved around the sun.

Influential people of his day yawned and nodded. They understood Copernicus in an abstract, intellectual sort of way. After all, his logic was overwhelming. Only a halfwit could dispute the evidence. But no one really accepted his theory at the gut level, because his discovery made no difference in anyone's life. It was rather ho-hum. The fact that the earth revolves around the sun seemed no more important than the fact that cats eat mice.

One day someone blurted, "Hey, wait a second! We can use all this in a new science called astronomy! Know what? We'll be able to navigate out there on the ocean! We'll be able to cut our unemployment by sending people to distant lands to encounter the heathen—to conquer, subjugate, and exploit. We'll be able to grab a lot of gold and silver and bring it back here! *That*'ll meet our existing needs and desires!"

The others stopped yawning. Someone else said, "Forget about the old stuff. We're going with that Polish kid Copernicus!" Once again, science marched on.

Moral: If you want to persuade people, show the immediate relevance and value of what you're saying in terms of meeting *their needs and desires*.

14. The power of attitude

Who's the worst person you can negotiate for?
Yourself.
You do a much better job negotiating for someone else.
Why?
Because you take yourself too seriously in any interaction that concerns *you*. You care too much about yourself. That puts you under pressure and stress. When you negotiate for someone else, you're more relaxed. You're more objective. You don't care as much, because you regard the situation as fun or as a game—*which it is*.

This characteristic of caring too much when we're personally involved is true with all of us. Recently I was asked to handle a large financial negotiation for a major bank overseas. The transaction involved millions of dollars, and everyone was uptight . . . except me. I was relaxed, enjoying the trip and thinking clearly. Do you know why I was so calm with so much at stake? It was the bankers who had the stake —not me. If everything went wrong they could lose millions, and were I them (knowing me as I do), I would have worried also. As for myself, I was getting paid by the day, so my attitude was, "Another day, another dollar." I viewed their big financial negotiation as a game—as fun. Oh, I cared—but I didn't care *that* much. Yet when I returned home to my daughter's report card, the games and fun were over. The family transaction around the kitchen table was serious, and because I cared so much I'm not so sure that I did as well at home as I had overseas.

Try to regard all encounters and situations, including your job, as a game, as the world of illusion. Pull back a little and enjoy it all. Do your best, but don't fall apart if everything doesn't pan out the way you'd like it to. Remember that things are seldom what they seem. Even skim milk masquerades as cream, and as Oscar Levant once said, "When you strip away the phony tinsel, what do you find underneath? The *real* tinsel."

Train yourself to say in every one of your negotiations, "If everything goes wrong, will my life end?" If the answer to this question is no, teach yourself to say, "Big deal," "Who cares?" and "So what?" Develop the attitude of caring —but not caring that much. To paraphrase Eugene O'Neill, "This episode is but a strange interlude in the electrical display of God the Father."

If you develop this healthy, somewhat amused, "it's a game" attitude toward all your negotiation encounters, both on and off the job, three benefits will follow.

1. You'll have considerably more energy, because you'll always have energy to do the things you enjoy doing. (You've undoubtedly experienced utter fatigue at the end of a grueling day, only to find the fatigue replaced

by explosive vitality when someone suggests you do something that you regard as a game—or fun.)

2. You'll be under reduced stress. There will be less uric acid in your bloodstream, and the tendency toward hypertension will diminish. You can even knock off some of the jogging you do, because your physical condition will improve. (If your job becomes fun, your anxiety will drop to the level you experience in a challenging game of Ping-Pong.)

3. You'll get better results, because your attitude will convey your feeling of power and mastery of your life. (You will transmit a confidence indicative of options, and people will start following you.)

Ironically, one of the more visible practitioners of this attitude is a media minister. The Reverend Ike, star of TV and radio, attracts a wide following with his message and unorthodox style. He preaches "green power" and frequently urges his audience to "Give God a great big hand."

One day he was walking among the people of his congregation and repeating over and over, "Don't worry. There's nothing to be concerned about."

A parishioner raised his hand and said, "Reverend Ike . . . you don't understand. I have a serious problem. I *am* worried."

The Reverend responded with cool demeanor, "Well, forget it."

"No, no! I can't . . . it's serious and I'm worried."

"So tell me," said the Reverend. "What could possibly trouble you so much?"

"It's the bank," declared the parishioner. "I owe the bank six thousand dollars. The loan is due tomorrow. I don't have any part of it, and I am really worried."

Reverend Ike didn't miss a beat. "My good man, why are *you* worried? It's that bank that has a serious problem!"

Although I have a nagging suspicion that the Reverend

Ike's guidance was a take-off on an old joke, there is a great deal to be said for this attitude.

We've put power under a magnifying glass. Now let us review again those three crucial variables present in every negotiation.

1. Power
2. Time
3. Information

It's time to look at time. . . .

*As long as you get there before
it's over you're never late.*
                    —James J. Walker

5. Time

It is an accepted truism that time marches on. It moves at the same rate for all of us, no matter what we do. Since we cannot control the clock, we must examine how the passage of time affects the negotiation process.

Most people speak of negotiation as though it were an event—something that has a definite beginning and ending. If this were so, it would have a fixed time frame. It might begin on a certain day at 9:00 A.M., when you have scheduled a meeting with your boss to ask about an overdue raise. Since his secretary told you that the boss has another appointment the following hour, you are aware of the time limitation. You believe your meeting will end at 10:00 A.M.

The following illustration depicts the starting point for this negotiation as G (when you enter the office) and the termination point as K (when he or she stands up to walk you to the door). It is this concluding point that we commonly call the deadline. How ominous that word sounds.

Assuming that this is an accurate portrayal, when will most concession behavior take place? At points G, H, I, or J? In virtually every negotiation, concessions will be made between points J and K, as close to the deadline as possible. Moreover, in almost all negotiations, agreements and settlements will not occur until point K (or possibly L), at or beyond the deadline.

In other words, if the boss acknowledges the merits of your case and finally agrees to grant the raise, it will probably happen at 9:55 A.M. This reality, that all the action occurs at the eleventh hour, holds true in every single negotiation:

When do most people file their income tax returns?

If a secretary is given seven days to type a report, when will it be completed?

Having two months to write a term paper, when will the student submit it? (Forget the submission, when will it be started?)

Even such a well-disciplined and responsible body as the U.S. Congress passes most of its legislation just prior to recess.

Therefore, in any negotiation expect most significant concession behavior and any settlement action to occur close to the deadline. That being the case, if I know your deadline and you don't know mine, who has the advantage? If you are a literalist about time (you believe it because you saw it in writing) and I'm flexible about time ("Hey, there's a deadline, and there's a *real* deadline") who will have the edge? Why, I will, because as we near the point that you perceive as the deadline, your stress level will increase, and you will make concessions.

As I watch you squirm, I can hold off yielding anything to you, even though my deadline is right after yours. The following will indicate how I learned this concept the hard way:

Twenty years ago, I was employed by a corporation that

was operating internationally. I had the type of key management position typified by my superiors' saying, "Hey, Cohen, how about two with cream and two with sugar!" To paraphrase Rodney Dangerfield, I didn't get no respect.

While fetching coffee for the biggies, I was exposed to those who had returned from overseas, brimming with exotic stories. Sometimes I'd meet them at breakfast before work. I'd ask, "Hey, where've you been?"

One would say, "Aw, just got back from Singapore, where I pieced together this nine-million-dollar deal."

Then turning to the other, I'd ask, "How about you?"

He'd say, "Oh, Abu Dhabi." I didn't even know where Abu Dhabi was.

Being polite they would ask, "Where've you been?"

What could I say? Well, I went to the zoo . . . the aquarium —but I'm looking forward to the botanic gardens. I had nothing to talk about. Since young people need "war stories," I used to go in to my boss every Friday. I begged him, over and over, "Give me a shot at the big time. Send me out there. Let me be a negotiator." I pestered him so much, he finally grunted, "Okay, Cohen—I'm going to send you to Tokyo to deal with the Japanese."

I was overjoyed. In my exhilaration, I told myself, "This is my moment! Destiny calls! I'll wipe out the Japanese, then move on to the rest of the international community."

One week later I was on a plane en route to Tokyo for the fourteen-day negotiation. I'd taken along all these books on the Japanese mentality, their psychology. I kept telling myself, "I'm really going to do well."

When the plane landed in Tokyo, I was the first passenger to trot down the ramp, raring to go. At the bottom of the ramp two Japanese gentlemen awaited me, bowing politely. I liked that.

The two Japanese helped me through customs, then escorted me to a large limousine I reclined comfortably on the plush seat at the rear of the limousine, and they sat stiffly on two fold-up stools. I said expansively, "Why don't you people join me? There's plenty of room back here."

They replied, "Oh, no—you're an important person. You obviously need your rest." I liked that, too.

As the limousine rolled along, one of my hosts asked, "By the way, do you know the language?"

I replied, "You mean Japanese?"

He said, "Right—that's what we speak in Japan."

I said, "Well, no, but I hope to learn a few expressions. I've brought a dictionary with me."

His companion asked, "Are you concerned about getting back to your plane on time?" (Up to that moment I had not been concerned.) "We can schedule this limousine to transport you back to the airport."

I thought to myself, "How considerate."

Reaching into my pocket, I handed them my return flight ticket, so the limousine would know when to get me. I didn't realize it then, but they knew my deadline, whereas I didn't know theirs.

Instead of beginning negotiations right away, they first had me experience Japanese hospitality and culture. For more than a week I toured the country from the Imperial Palace to the shrines of Kyoto. They even enrolled me in an English-language course in Zen to study their religion.

Every evening for four and a half hours, they had me sit on a cushion on a hardwod floor for a traditional dinner and entertainment. Can you imagine what it's like sitting on a hardwood floor for all those hours? If I didn't get hemorrhoids as a result, I'll probably never get them. Whenever I inquired about the start of negotiations, they'd murmur, "Plenty of time! Plenty of time!"

At last, on the twelfth day, we began the negotiations, finishing early so we could play golf. On the thirteenth day, we began again, and ended early because of the farewell dinner. Finally, on the morning of the fourteenth day, we resumed our negotiating in earnest. Just as we were getting to the crux of things, the limousine pulled up to take me to the airport. We all piled in and continued hashing out the terms. Just as the limousine's brakes were applied at the terminal, we consummated the deal.

How well do you think I did in that negotiation? For many years my superiors referred to it as "The first great Japanese victory since Pearl Harbor."

Why did the debacle occur? Because my hosts knew my deadline and I didn't know theirs. They held off making concessions, correctly anticipating that I wouldn't allow myself to go home empty handed. Furthermore, the impatience that I undoubtedly displayed conveyed my belief that this departure deadline was somehow sacred. As if this would be the last plane to leave Tokyo for all time.

Even the most experienced negotiators occasionally fall for a similar ploy. For example, do you remember when the United States wanted to extricate itself from the Vietnam War?

We tried for months to get the North Vietnamese to the bargaining table. For months we used direct appeals and intermediaries. All to no avail.

In effect, what they were saying was, "We've been fighting this war for 627 years. What does it matter if we fight another 128? In fact, a 32-year war would be a quickie for us!" Americans couldn't believe it. A 32-year quickie!

Did the North Vietnamese literally mean that? Of course not. Did they have a deadline? Yes, just as the Japanese did when I dealt with them in Tokyo. Were they are under pressure to conclude at least this phase of the conflict? Certainly. But they perpetuated their bluff because they knew that Americans were not committed to an indefinite struggle in Southeast Asia.

After months of continued hostilities, the North Vietnamese finally relented. Just prior to an American presidential election, they agreed to hold peace talks in Paris. The United

States quickly dispatched Averell Harriman as our representative, and he rented a room on a week-to-week basis in the Ritz Hotel at the Place Vendôme in the center of the city.

Do you remember what the North Vietnamese did? They eventually rented a villa outside of Paris with a two-and-a-half-year lease. Do you think that this North Vietnamese attitude about time, later compounded by endless disputes over the shape of the bargaining table, had an impact on the outcome of the negotiations? Emphatically it did. In retrospect we can now understand why the Paris peace accords never successfully resolved the war—at least, to our satisfaction.

In spite of their seeming devil-may-care attitude about time, the North Vietnamese *did* have a deadline. Take it from me, as an article of faith, that the other side—*every* "other side" —*always* has a deadline. If they didn't have some pressure to negotiate, you would not be able to find them. But time and time again, the other side tries to act nonchalant—and the nonchalant posture is effective. It works because you feel the pressure of your own time constraints, which always appear greater than theirs. This is true in all negotiation encounters.

Do you recall the Sears refrigerator salesman who returns periodically with a greeting of, "Hi, there—made up your mind?" Chances are that beneath his calm façade lies an anxiety-ridden human being whose boss told him that very morning, "If you don't sell a refrigerator today, tomorrow you'll be out in the elements pumping gas on an island."

Here's another article of faith you can hang your hat on: Deadlines—your own and other people's—are more flexible than you realize. Who gives you your deadlines? Who imposes them on you? Essentially, you yourself, in an activity called self-discipline or managing your time. Your boss, the government, a customer, or a family member may have something to do with it, but primarily *your deadline is of your own making.*

Since this is the case, you never need blindly follow a

deadline. I'm not saying you should ignore deadlines. I am saying you should analyze them. Since they are invariably the products of a negotiation they might well be negotiable.

Always ask yourself, "What will happen if I go beyond the deadline? What is the certainty of the detriment or penalty? What is the extent of the punishment? In short, how great is the risk I'm taking?"

For instance, we all know that the deadline for filing your income-tax return in the United States is April 15. What happens when you file late? Will someone pound on your door with a rifle butt and drag you off for incarceration? Hardly.

If you analyze this deadline, a yardstick for your behavior might be whether you owe the government money or whether the government owes you. If you are a substantial debtor who files really late, the Internal Revenue Service will penalize you, charging you interest and a penalty on the sum owed. However, if you compare the rate of return that the government is getting for allowing you to use their money to the rate that banks charge for a comparable loan, you'll find that the government's terms may be more favorable.

The real question should be, "To whom do you want to give your business, the local bank at a high rate or the United States government at a reasonable rate?" Myself, I say, "Go with Uncle Sam!"

What happens if the government owes you money and you file your return late? Although you may have to wait a little longer for the refund, there is no penalty. Why, the IRS is lucky you aren't charging them interest. Yet people who know they will have a refund coming knock themselves out to get the magical postmark prior to midnight, April 15. Some of them goof up their computations because of last-minute haste and end up being subjected to a costly, time-consuming audit.

Ask yourself, "If the government owes me money, why am I running?" Then say to yourself, "I'll go over my return leisurely, double-check the arithmetic, and then drop it off at the post office when it's convenient to do so."

As we have seen, the way we view and use time can be crucial to success. Time may even affect a relationship. A delayed arrival may be seen as evidence of confidence or hostility, whereas an early arrival may be viewed as anxiety or a lack of consideration for others. Time can favor either side, depending on the circumstances. Regardless of these interim interpretations which may affect the negotiation climate, some of the observations already made are worth repeating:

1. Since most concession behavior and settlements will occur at or even beyond the deadline, be patient. True strength often calls for the ability to sustain the tension without flight or fight. Learn to keep your automatic defense responses under control. Remain calm but keep alert for the favorable moment to act. As a general rule, *patience pays*. It may be that the thing to do, when you do not know what to do, is to do nothing.

2. In an adversary negotiation your best strategy is not to reveal your real deadine to the other side. Always keep in mind that since deadlines are the product of a negotiation they are more flexible than most people realize. Never blindly follow a deadline but evaluate the benefits and detriments that will ensue as you approach, or go beyond, the brink.

3. The "other side," cool and serene as they may appear, always have a deadline. Most often, the tranquillity they display outwardly masks a great deal of stress and pressure.

4. Precipitous action should be taken only when it's guaranteed to be to your advantage. Generally speaking, you cannot achieve the best outcome quickly; you can achieve it only slowly and perseveringly. Very often as you approach the deadline a shift of

power will occur, presenting a creative solution or even a turnaround by the other side. The people may not change, but with the passage of time, circumstances do.

Having examined *power* and *time,* let's move to the next ingredient: *information. . . .*

Some people feel the rain;
others just get wet.
                    —Roger Miller

6. Information

Information is the heart of the matter. It can unlock the door to the vault called success. It affects our appraisal of reality and the decisions that we make. Why then do we fail to get adequate information? Because we tend to regard our negotiation encounters with people as a limited happening or an event. We seldom anticipate that we will need information until the occurrence of a crisis or a "focal event," which creates a cascade of dysfunctional consequences.

Only under emergency circumstances and a pressing deadline do we see ourselves as embarking upon a negotiation. Suddenly, we are in the boss's office, entering the car dealership, or about to greet the Sears refrigerator salesman. Of course, obtaining information under these conditions presents enormous difficulties.

In discussing *time* we saw how the end of a negotiation is more flexible than most people realize. Similarly, the actual starting point of a negotiation always precedes the face-to-face happening by weeks or even months. As you read this book, you are in the "process stage" of many negotiations that won't take place for some time yet.

Therefore, a negotiation—or any meaningful interaction— isn't an *event,* it's a *process.* If you'll pardon the analogy, a negotiation is like a performance appraisal or mental illness, neither of which has a precisely defined time segment. For example, if a psychiatrist declares that a patient is mentally ill on Friday, June 6, at 4:00 P.M., does that mean the patient becomes ill at that precise moment? Does it mean that the patient is perfectly normal at 3:59 P.M. and suddenly goes bananas sixty seconds later? Of course not. He or she has developed symptoms long before then. Mental illness is a process occurring over an extended period.

During the actual negotiating event it is often common strategy for one or both sides to conceal their true interests, needs, and priorities. Their rationale is that information is power, particularly in situations where you cannot trust the other side fully. Old horse traders never let the seller know which horse really interests them, because if they did the price might go up. Of course, it would give you a big advantage if you could learn what the other side really want, their limits, and their deadline. Your chances of getting this information from an experienced negotiator during the event in an adversary transaction are very remote.

How do you gather this information? You start early, because the earlier you start, the easier it is to obtain information. You always get more information *preceding* an acknowledged, formal confrontation, because people willingly let their hair down before the red light glows on the TV camera, to use a figure of speech. Once the red light glows, their attitude becomes defensive. They say, "Come on . . . I can't tell you anything now—it's negotiation time!"

During the information-gathering period prior to the negotiation event, you quietly and consistently probe. You do *not* come on like a grand inquisitor but rather as a humble human being—a regular Joe or Sally, complete with "pimples."

Some of us assume that the more intimidating or flawless we appear to others, the more they will tell us. Actually, the opposite is true. The more confused and defenseless you seem, the more readily they will help you with information and advice. So leave your bank-loan suit home and forget the makeup; a visible pimple or two won't hurt. With this approach you will find it easy to listen more than talk. You should prefer asking questions to giving answers. In fact you ask questions even when you think you know the answers, because by doing so, you test the credibility of the other side.

From whom do you glean and gather information? From anyone who works with or for the person you will meet with during the event or anyone who has dealt with them in the past. This includes secretaries, clerks, engineers, janitors, spouses, technicians, or past customers. They will willingly respond to you if you use a nonthreatening approach.

In many years of negotiation, again and again people have told me rewarding things. One summer I had a job in sales, and I remember a foreman's mentioning in an informal conversation, "Your product is the only one that passed our tests and meets our specifications," and "Hey, Cohen! When do you think we'll conclude next month's negotiation? We're running out of inventory!" Obviously I tucked all this information away and then remembered it when face to face during the actual negotiating with the purchasing manager.

Realistically, it may not always be possible for you to make this direct contact with the other side's associates. On these occasions you can make use of third parties, use the telephone, or speak with people who have negotiated with them in the past. Everyone has a track record, and you can learn from the experience of others.

Another source of data is your adversary's competitors, who may well be willing to talk to you about costs. If you, as a buyer, can gain access to the seller's costs, you will have a tremendous bargaining advantage. This information is not as difficult to obtain as you might think, since many publications, both private (for example the automobile *Blue Book*) and governmental, furnish all sorts of data upon request.

Remember, what you want to know going into the negotiation event is the real limits on the other side, that is, the extent beyond which they will not go. The more information you have about their financial situation, priorities, deadlines, costs, real needs, and organizational pressures, the better you can bargain. And the sooner you start to acquire these data, the easier they will be to obtain.

In most instances, there's more to gathering information than playing humble and saying, "Help me." Generally you have to give information in order to get some in return. You gradually give selective information for three reasons:

1. According to the Bible, it's more blessed to give than to receive.
2. Perceptive people won't communicate with you beyond the chit-chat level until reciprocal risks take place. They won't share information with you until you share some commensurate information with them. To persuade someone to advance to another square, you have to advance to another square, seemingly on an even-Steven basis with their revelations. This is mutual risk-taking behavior—the deliberate building of two-way trust.
3. When you give carefully worded and controlled information during the "process stage," you hope to lower the expectation level of the other side.

This third point is especially important because if you spring something completely new during the event, the response you receive will be, "No way—I never heard of that." If your surprise is close to the deadline you have a strong chance of deadlocking the negotiation. However, if you were to introduce the same new concept early during the "process stage," then raise it several more times, at adroitly spaced intervals, the concept would become familiar to the other side. If this matter were now brought up during the event, the response might well be, "Oh, that—it's been around for a while." In essence it takes some time to get used to any new idea. Because it's now familiar, it's somehow acceptable.

Don't be surprised, therefore, when you receive the initial rejection to your new request prior to the event. "No" is a reaction, not a position. The people who react negatively to your proposal simply need time to evaluate it and adjust their thinking. With the passage of sufficient time and repeated efforts on your part, almost every "no" can be transformed into a "maybe" and eventually a "yes." If you allow a sufficient period for acceptance time and can furnish them with the new information that they have not considered in formulating their initial "no," you can win them over.

An example of this was the American public's initial reaction toward the impeachment of President Richard Nixon. When this idea was first raised, a survey was taken of sixteen hundred people, presumably a cross-section of the electorate. The reaction was 92 percent against, and the reasons given were: "I never heard of this before," "Why, it would weaken the office of the presidency," and "It would serve as a bad precedent for future generations."

Three months later another poll was taken of the same people, and those not in favor of the proposition dropped to 80 percent. After the passage of a few more months the same respondents were 68 percent against impeachment. When the final interviews were conducted, less than a year after these people were first contacted, 60 percent were *for* the impeachment of the president.

How come all those people changed their minds? Obviously there were two reasons:

1. They had received additional information.
2. They had become used to what originally was a new idea.

Remember that change and new ideas are acceptable only when presented slowly in bite-size fragments. Keep that in mind when trying to alter someone's viewpoint, thinking, perceptions, and expectations. For most people, it's easier and more comfortable to stay in the groove. The fact that the difference between a rut and a groove is just a matter of degree doesn't seem to bother them. Only through perseverance can you hope to change them and implement your goals.

When you finally arrive at the negotiating event, you must discipline yourself to practice effective listening techniques. If you are carefully concentrating on what's going on, you can learn a great deal about the other side's feelings, motivation, and real needs. Of course, attentive listening and observation mean not just hearing what is being said, but also understanding what is being omitted. People are reluctant to lie outright, but some are not hesitant to fudge, circumvent, or evade. When you begin to hear generalities, that's your cue to start asking specific questions in order to clarify what is actually being said.

The study and interpretation of cues has become very popular in recent years. A cue is a message sent indirectly whose meaning may be ambiguous and require interpretation. Essentially they fall into three basic categories:

1. *Unintentional Cues*, in which behavior or words transmit an inadvertent message (for example, the Freudian slip);
2. *Verbal Cues*, in which voice intonation or emphasis sends a message that seems to contradict the words being spoken;
3. *Behavioral Cues*, which are the language of the body as displayed in posture, facial expressions, eye contact, and hand gestures, where a person sits at a conference table, who nudges whom or who pats whom on the shoulder (presumably, in our culture, pattors have more power than pattees).

To further explain what we mean by behavioral cues or "nonverbal vibes," let me set the scene. A husband has been away on a business trip for an extended period. He has lived an ascetic life on the road, and longing has built up in his heart. Walking toward his house, suitcase in hand, he notices that the lights are somewhat dim. Moving closer he hears soft music emanating from the house. He quickens his pace as anxiety begins to build. Then he notices a woman, who appears to be his wife, standing in the doorway in a diaphanous gown, a martini in each hand.

He calls out to her, "Where are the kids?"

She responds, "They won't be home for hours." Now I ask you, is that a cue or is that a cue? To some of us the cue may be that we're in the wrong house!

The point is that we all live in a world where nonverbal signals are being transmitted and received. How does a wife tell a husband that tonight's *the night,* when ordinarily it's not the night? Does she write him a memo, "Re: Activities for the evening—please disregard prior schedule"? Conversely, how does a wife inform a husband that tonight's *not* the night, when ordinarily it is? The latter is a more familiar occurrence for some of us.

From the time we were infants, we all learned to communicate our needs, likes, and dislikes to others without resorting to words. This ability has remained with us, and it often appears in the form of a raised eyebrow, a smile, a touch, a scowl, a wink, or a reluctance to make eye contact during a conversation. These actions are all behavioral cues, or a form of body language.

People have become fascinated with the art of sending and decoding nonverbal messages (reading behavioral cues), as evidenced by the growing number of published writings and lectures on the subject. Authorities have even given legitimacy to this field by labeling it the science of proxemics—the study of space and the movement of people within it. As for the value of this wordless language in negotiation, it is definitely limited. The interpretation of most body language is obvious; nevertheless, it may be misleading to ascribe some universal meaning to an isolated gesture, regardless of the circumstances.

Here's an example of a situation in which the interpretation is rather obvious. Because of an unexpected early-morning errand, you get a delayed start for work. Arriving out of breath, you notice that the boss is sitting at your desk. As you approach, he leans back in your chair, puts his hands behind his head, and spreads his elbows wide. With his eyes on the wall clock he casually remarks, "Do you know what time it is?" Assuming that the boss can tell time, you don't have to be an expert to know what's going on.

As for trying to catalog and give meaning to each and every body gesture, the following example should suffice. Assume that you are trying to sell me a service or a product, and in the middle of the sales pitch I begin to stroke my chin with my thumb and forefinger. What does that mean? Have I decided to buy or not? I don't think *anyone* has *any* idea what it means. Freud wouldn't have known what it meant. It may indicate that I have a pimple, that I cut myself while shaving, that I'm trying to make a cleft like Cary Grant's, that I'm trying to cover my double chin, or that I have a neuromuscular habit that I'm unaware of.

Although I'm saying that trying to interpret one single cue in isolation is a waste of time, a sensitivity to what is really being communicated is important. If some people have become paranoid about picking up on nonverbal vibes, more people are completely literal. These are the audio-visual types who believe only what they can see and hear. Invariably they say things like, "Let's put it in writing," "Around here we go by the book," and finally, "Why am I the last to know?" When literalists see the "handwriting on the wall," they don't even read the message but closely examine the penmanship. To paraphrase H. L. Mencken, a literalist is one who, upon observing that a rose smells better than a cabbage, concludes that it will also make better soup.

As a negotiator, you must be sensitive to the nonverbal factors in any communication. Even Saint Paul advised, "The letter kills, but the spirit gives life." So during the negotiation event, force yourself to step back so you can listen with your "third ear" and observe with your "third eye." This detachment will enable you to hear the words in their proper non-verbal context and enable you to see the pattern. In negotiation, cues are meaningful if they are part of a cluster and indicate the direction of movement.

To show the significance of cues if they are seen as a part of a pattern, I give you this case in point. Let's say you are trying to sell an idea to your boss. As you start your explanation, you're aware that the boss is staring out the window at a telephone pole. That's a cue that in and of itself may mean nothing, like my rubbing my chin. You continue your discourse. Now the boss leans back in his chair, constructs a steeple with his fingertips, and squints at you through the steeple. That's another cue. But in conjunction with the first cue, it may be meaningful. Nevertheless, you continue to pitch away. The boss starts drumming his desk-top with his left index finger. That's another cue, continuing to form a pattern with the preceding two. Does the finger tapping mean, "Keep up the good work! You're doing fine!" Hardly. A literalist would probably think, "Hey, my boss has got a Latin American beat!"

Now the boss stands up, puts his arm around your shoulders, and begins to edge you toward the door. That's still another cue. If you're halfway perceptive, the cue pattern is glaringly observable. (A literalist would ask himself, "What's the story? Why this sudden affection? What's this person trying to pull? I thought he had a family!") But it is to be hoped that you aren't a literalist. By this time you're at the door, the boss's eyes are opaque, and he's nodding goodbye.

I'm obviously exaggerating here, but my point is that the big advantage in reading cues is that in a cluster they furnish feedback concerning how you are progressing toward your goal. If the pattern is not to your liking, you can use your lead time (before you get to the door) to make the necessary adjustments.

How can we apply all this to a negotiating situation? The key piece of information that any negotiator would like to have about the other party is their real limits or just how much they will sacrifice to make this deal. In other words, what is the lowest price that the seller will sell for, or what is the absolute top figure that the buyer will pay? Very often this can be ascertained by observing the pattern of concession behavior on the part of the other side.

Suppose that I'm negotiating with you to purchase some expensive stereo equipment that contains advanced technology new in the marketplace. Let's say for the sake of argument that all I have in my budget is $1,500. Since your product is new, you would like to get as much as you can to test what the customer demand might be for this sophisticated technology.

If my first offer to you is $1,000, and my next offer is $1,400, how much money will you assume I have in my budget? If our relationship is that of adversaries with little trust, you may well anticipate that I actually have $1,600, $1,800, or even $2,000 to spend. Why? Because the increment between $1,000 and $1,400 is so great that you probably will expect that I have more than $1,500. Even if I swear that I have only $1,500, and it happens to be true, you are not likely to believe me in a perceived competitive transaction. This is valid because we all tend to disregard the protestations of the other side. Our experience teaches us that the increments of concession behavior are the most accurate barometer of the true limits of authorization.

Accordingly, if the environment for negotiations is competitive, you see me as an adversary, and in order to achieve a collaborative result, I will have to play the competitive game. In this climate here's how I should let you know that $1,500 is my ceiling. I make an initial offer of $900, which you reject. My next tender is $1,200. Then I extend myself to $1,350. After some delay I go to $1,425. The next advance is to a reluctant $1,433.62. It is easier to get you to believe I have $1,500 this way, because I have steadily decreased the increments instead of acting like a drunken sailor. Creeping upward as I just did is known as playing the "monetary-increment game."

Some of you reading this book who are disciples of Howard Cosell may say, "I don't like to play games. Why can't I just tell it like it is?" Certainly that's your prerogative, but remember that in order *to achieve a collaborative result in a competitive environment, you have to play the game.* If you don't want to do this, you have an alternative: You can change the climate of our relationship to build trust between us. To the extent that you are successful, you can minimize the gaming. My point is merely that you take your reality as it actually is and must always operate in accordance with that reality. So to repeat: To achieve a collaborative result in an adversary environment, you have to play the competitive game.

This brings to mind an amusing experience I had with someone who *didn't* play the "monetary-increment game." I have a neighbor who's a medical doctor, a "professional person." (The definition of a professional person is someone who likes to make money but not to talk about it.) When his home sustained storm damage, he rang my front-door bell and said, "Herb, do me a favor, will you? A claims adjuster is coming over to haggle about money. You deal with this sort of thing all the time. Would you mind talking to him for me?"

I said, "Sure, I'd be glad to. How much would you like to get?"

He replied, "See if the insurance company will pay $300, okay?"

I nodded, then asked, "Tell me, what did the storm loss cost you out of pocket?"

He replied, "I lost more than $300—that's for sure!"

I said, "All right, what if I can get you $350?"

He said, "Oh, $350 would be fantastic!"

What I had done was to get his commitment to an objective in order to avoid the possibility of Monday-morning quarter-backing on his part.

A half hour later, the claims adjuster rang my doorbell. When I ushered him into my living room, he opened his attaché case and said, "Mr. Cohen, I know a person like you is accustomed to dealing with big numbers. I'm afraid I don't have much for you here. How would you feel about a *first offer* of *only* $100?"

I was silent for a moment, but the blood drained from my face. You see, I've been programmed and conditioned to respond to all first offers by blurting the equivalent of, "Are you out of your cotton-picking mind? Are you *crazy?* I can't accept *that!*" Besides, I learned in early puberty that a first offer *always* implies a second and maybe even a third. More-over, when he uses the word "only," it means that he himself is embarrassed in mentioning such a paltry sum, so how am I supposed to feel as the recipient of such an offer?

After I snorted my disbelief, the adjuster muttered, "All right, I'm sorry. Forget what I just said. How about a little more, like $200?"

I responded, "A little more? Absolutely no."

He continued, "All right then, what about $300?"

After a slight pause I said, "$300? Gee . . . I don't know."

He swallowed and said, "Okay, make that $400."

I said, "$400. Gee . . . I don't know."

He said, "Okay . . . make that $500."

I said, "$500? Gee . . . I don't know."

He said, "All right . . . make that $600."

Now I ask you, what do you think I will say now? Yes, you guessed it: "$600? Gee . . . I don't know." Why do I keep saying, "Gee . . . I don't know"? Gee . . . I don't know—but it's working like crazy. I'm afraid to say anything else!

The claim was finally settled for $950, and I went next door to get the release signed. My neighbor greeted me with, "How did we do?" and I blurted out, "Gee . . . I don't know."

To this day, I'm not so sure that I did that well in this negotiation, because the adjuster's unintentional cueing blew my mind. *Moral:* Watch the increments of concession behavior, since they send a strong message about the real limits of authority.

PART THREE

STYLES OF NEGOTIATING

*Never get angry. Never make
a threat. Reason with people.*
> —Don Corleone
> *The Godfather*

A few years ago during a plane trip, my seat partner asked, "What do you do for a living?"

I replied, "I'm a negotiator."

My companion got a glimmer in his eye and tried to suppress an all-knowing smile. From his reaction I knew what he was thinking: "Well, what do you know? This guy probably sells aluminum siding to tenants residing in brick apartment houses."

Unfortunately, this negative reaction to the word "negotiator" is a misconception shared by a great many people. When they hear it they automatically think of a slick manipulator who is attempting to win at the expense of some innocent victim. Certainly, there are those who operate this way. However, this competitive strategy is only one approach to getting what you want. Actually, the style of negotiators can cover a broad range along a continuum between those who are competitive (I win, you lose) and those who are collaborative (both of us can win).

We now focus on these two primary modes of negotiating behavior that individuals use for conflict resolution:

In Chapter 7, "Winning at All Costs . . . Soviet Style," negotiators try to get what they want at the expense of the other side. Even if you never use this strategy, you should have the ability to recognize it; otherwise, you may be victimized by it.

Then, in Chapters 8 and 9, "Negotiating for Mutual Satisfaction," and "More on the Win-Win Technique," the emphasis shifts from the effort to defeat an opponent to the effort to defeat a problem and achieve a mutually accepted outcome. Here everyone is working together to find a creative solution that will meet the needs of both sides.

*The meek shall inherit the earth
—but not its mineral rights.*

—J. Paul Getty

7. Winning at all costs ...
Soviet style

Alfred P. Doolittle sings in *My Fair Lady,*

> *The Lord above made man to help his neighbor
> No matter where—on land or sea or foam—
> But with a little bit of luck,
> When he comes around, you won't be home.*

The song is supposedly British, but the lyrics, written by Alan Jay Lerner, could apply to almost any western culture. To many people this is a competitive world in which one's success is measured not by how well you have done compared to your potential but by how many you have outdistanced. We all live in a society pervaded by potential Win-Lose situations in which the competitive struggle for admission to a "good college" can be just as rugged as the competition between McDonald's and Burger King.

Some people interpret this to mean that all life is a constant battle of winning and losing. They see a world filled with rivals and competitors, with persons who want their job, their class standing, their money, their promotion, their parking space, their place in line, or their spouse.

The competitive negotiator sees almost everything as a constant struggle of winning and losing. He is a tough battler who seeks to meet his own goals at all costs without worrying about the needs and the acceptance of others. There is no doubt in his mind that he is right in his conviction and approach. For such a person each victory brings a sense of exhilaration.

Although such a view and strategy have limited application, there are some people who constantly employ this style without making a distinction between an associate and a true adversary. Though they may be concerned only with their own winning, the resulting outcome is the defeat of the other side. If their relationship is a continuing one, the outcome of this negotiation leaves a legacy that will affect the future relations of the parties.

The competitive (Win-Lose) approach occurs when someone or some group attempts to achieve their objective at the expense of a perceived adversary. These attempts to triumph *over* an opponent may run the gamut from blatant efforts at intimidation to subtle forms of manipulation. I call this self-oriented strategy the "Soviet style." This term is descriptive, because more than anyone else, the Soviet Union's leaders consistently try to win at the expense of other nations or groups.

Don't get me wrong. I'm not referring to a national or ethnic way of interacting. I'm talking about a negotiation style that has nothing to do with geography. There are people with excellent local pedigree, people we all encounter, who try to operate Soviet style

How do you spot these Win-Lose negotiators? Obviously they try never to tip their hands. They're much too slick to unmask themselves as "Soviets." Seemingly humble and considerate, they appear concerned about your needs. They confront you with a smile on their lips and a twinkle in their eyes. They figuratively carry a Bible in their left hand and tote holy water in a hip flask. With their right hand they bless you, then benignly murmur, "Go in peace, my son!" Only after they've left do you notice a trickle of blood running down your leg. Only then do you have difficulty removing your coat because of the stiletto in your back. Only then do you mutter, "Son of a gun! *Soviet!*"

After they are gone and you become aware of the damages they have inflicted, it is difficult to do much. Again, the question: How do you recognize the Soviet style? You distinguish it by the specific behavior of the other side. All "Soviets," whether from Moscow or from Memphis, use the same six steps in their negotiation dance:

1. *Extreme intitial positions.* They always start with tough demands or ridiculous offers that affect the other side's expectation level.
2. *Limited authority.* The negotiators themselves have little or no authority to make any concessions.
3. *Emotional tactics.* They get red faced, raise their voices, and act exasperated—horrified that they are being taken advantage of. Occasionally they will stalk out of a meeting in a huff.
4. *Adversary concessions viewed as weakness.* Should you give in and concede them something, they are unlikely to reciprocate.
5. *Stingy in their concessions.* They delay making any concession and when they finally do, it reflects only a minuscule change in their position.
6. *Ignore deadlines.* They tend to be patient and act as though time is of no significance to them.

Having outlined the six-step Soviet style, let me now elaborate on each of these points with specific examples and analogies:

1. Extreme initial positions

Whenever purchasing an expensive (big-ticket) item, they will make a paltry first offer. Usually this is done in secret, behind closed doors, to prevent additional buyers from bidding. The tactic is used to make the seller believe that there is no available option other than dealing with them. For example, when did we learn about the Soviet purchase of Canadian or American wheat? Usually after the tonnage had been loaded on special tankers for overseas shipment. In some places these transactions were referred to as The Great Grain Robbery.

Here's another instance of how the Soviets operate as buyers: Almost thirty years ago they were interested in securing a large parcel of land on the North Shore of Long Island. They intended to build a recreational center for their embassy personnel. At that time, acreage the size they wanted in this area was selling between $360,000 and $500,000. The property they decided on was appraised at $420,000.

Did the cagey Russians offer to pay $420,000, or even $360,000? Not on your life. Since they're past masters at "lowballing," they made an initial offer of $125,000—a laughable figure. But no one laughed. How did the Soviets get away with this? They did what they always do when purchasing: Negotiating in secret, they eliminated possible competition.

In this case they paid a small amount for an exclusive one-year option to buy with the proviso that the matter be kept secret. The owners of the property knew that the $125,000 figure was ludicrous. However, they were unable to get other offers because of the secrecy restriction. After three months of token haggling and frustration, they muttered in effect, "We know this is ridiculous, but maybe we were a *little* high." So they dropped the asking price from $420,000 to $360,000. Psychologically, the Soviets had set them up like pawns on a chess board.

When the Soviets are sellers of anything substantial, they do just the opposite. They make excessive demands, then fling the doors wide open to encourage competitive bidding. By playing various bidders against each other and egging them on to outdo each other, they escalate the final agreed-upon selling price to stratospheric levels.

A graphic illustration of this method can be seen in the sale of the rights to televise the 1980 Olympics from Moscow (before the United States boycotted the Olympics and made the matter academic.).

The cost of these rights has risen considerably from what CBS paid for the 1960 Olympics in Rome to ABC's winning bid for the Montreal games in 1976. The approximate selling prices follow:

1960	one-half million dollars
1964	three million dollars
1968	five million dollars
1972	thirteen million dollars
1976	twenty-two million dollars

The Soviets, with typical guile, smashed this predictable succession pattern. During the summer games in Montreal, the top brass of all three networks were invited to a lavish party on board the *Alexander Pushkin,* which was moored in the St. Lawrence River. Each network was contacted separately and given the Soviet demand: They wanted $210 million—in cash! Their asking price did not exactly follow a geometric progression.

Generating cut-throat in-fighting, they did what I mentioned earlier: They encouraged competitive bidding. Inviting representatives of ABC, NBC, and CBS to the Soviet capital, they essentially reduced them to three gladiators hacking at each other in a Roman arena. Roone Arledge, then head of ABC Sports, bitterly commented, "They want us to be like three scorpions fighting in a bottle. When it's over, two will be dead and the winner will be exhausted."

I witnessed part of this struggle between the minions of Moscow and the moguls of Manhattan. I was in the Soviet Union at the time, embroiled in negotiations of a different nature. I attended one of the cocktail parties thrown to keep the gladiators' spirits up. Never have I sipped better vodka, nibbled tastier caviar, or seen more strained and determined faces.

As they entered the stretch, here was the bidding: NBC, $70 million; CBS $71 million; and ABC had come up to $73 million. It was generally assumed at the time, that the experience of ABC in broadcasting eight of ten prior Olympics would give them the edge. However, CBS hired the services of Lothar Bock, a professional go-between from Munich, Germany. With the help of Bock a meeting was arranged between the Soviet negotiators and William S. Paley, the Chairman of CBS, in November 1976. On this occasion a deal was struck, with CBS agreeing to raise its bid one more time and offering even more concessions.

Everyone asumed that CBS had won out over its competition. However, the Soviets could not resist the "nibble," and early in December 1976 they announced another round of bidding. The CBS executives were upset but went back to Moscow for the showdown, which was to take place on December 15. At that time the Soviets announced to the three networks that what had occurred up to that point merely qualified each of them to enter the final stage of the auction. The Americans were appalled by the impudence of their hosts, and despite Soviet threats, they all dropped out and went home.

This left the Soviet negotiators empty handed. To be left empty handed in the U.S.S.R. is to be in big trouble. When American officials negotiate and goof up, their livelihoods may be affected. When Soviet officials negotiate and goof up, their *lives* may be affected.

Desperate to generate fresh competition, the Soviets came up with a fourth option. They proclaimed that the rights to televise the Olympics now belonged to an obscure American trading company named SATRA, which had an office in New York City. SATRA is *not* what anyone might call a media conglomerate. Granting the rights to them was equivalent to telling a kid who owns a Polaroid, "Do a good job, sonny—the Olympics are yours."

Cleverly using SATRA leverage, the Soviets induced Lothar Bock to recontact the networks. He did and eventually offered his connections and services to NBC. Wheedling, wheeling and dealing, and flying back and forth between Moscow and Manhattan, Bock ultimately peddled the rights to televise the Olympics to NBC for $87 million. On top of that sum, the network agreed to pay Bock roughly $6 million for his services, plus additional sums for entertainment specials. Of course, subsequent events caused NBC to regret this victory over their arch-rivals. (Note: The Soviets were never serious about their excessive demand of $210 million. It was later learned that they expected the rights to be sold for between $60 million and $70 million.)

Although the cited examples actually involve the Soviet Union, similar tactics have long been used in our society. Many years ago I worked for a large casualty insurance company that had a publicized claim philosophy that stated, "Prompt, fair settlement of all just claims, with courtesy and consideration for all."

In spite of these lofty sentiments the system rewarded adjusters who lowballed claimants with meager first offers in the best Kremlin tradition. This tactic worked because the recipients mistakenly believed that they had no other option but to deal with the adjuster, who represented a monopoly position. Of course, they had other options: Complain to the state Department of Insurance, write to the president of the insurance company, go over the adjuster's head to personally visit the claims manager, pursue this matter in small-claims court, retain an attorney to represent them, or even just wait for the pressure of time to take its toll on their adversary.

Situations where the asking price is excessive and intense competition is generated among prospective buyers should also sound familiar. It can be seen at auctions everywhere, with bidders pitted against each other in the fiercest sort of price haggling. Whenever you have a scarce product, commodity, or service, sellers have been known to exploit the greed of prospective buyers who want instant gratification of their needs. A number of years ago the Mazda RX 7, an imported Japanese automobile, was in such hot demand that some dealers orchestrated a flurry of bids and counter-bids that resulted in this car's selling for as much as $2,000 more than its listed price.

Why do these Win-Lose Soviet tactics work? Because we let them work. We are influenced by the extreme initial position, and we're further baffled when the people we negotiate with seem to lack authority.

2. Limited authority

Let's say that I am a representative of International Harvester and I have been entrusted with the authority to go to the Soviet Union to sell them tractors. If the Soviets are interested, I will ultimately meet with some tough, experienced negotiators from one of their government's foreign-trade agencies. These are not the people who will oversee the use of my product and certainly not those who will make the decision on whether to buy. Because everything in the Soviet Union is determined by a select few in the Politburo, the people sitting across the table from me for three months have no discretionary authority to make any concessions or agreements.

What is the effect of this dilemma? I have adequate authority to consummate a deal, but my adversaries always have to consult with some absent commissar to make any movement. If they have no authority, what happens when we interact over a period of time? I may make offers and concessions, whereas they only give me vodka and comradeship.

Having been away a long time, I have a compulsion to make *some* headway. As a result, I continue to make offers. What am I doing? I am bidding against myself. That's why you should never negotiate with anyone totally lacking in authority. The only exception might be when you're very lonely. Presumably, you would then be negotiating for something else, which may be beyond the scope of this book.

A variation of this gimmick is frequently practiced by car dealers, who give limited authority to their salespeople on the showroom floor. Invariably the person you're dealing with will always excuse himself to speak to the sales manager and even on occasion to the owner of the dealership. He may or may not speak to anyone, but he uses the time to help him evaluate the negotiation.

Many years ago during a particularly cold Chicago winter, I found myself on a used-car lot searching for a second auto. Since the temperature was below freezing, I made an offer and was anxious to conclude the purchase. To my amusement, the individual I was dealing with claimed a lack of authority at that price and said, "One moment, please. I'll have to speak to the guy in the shack." Now I ask you, do you believe anyone is actually in that shack? Could anyone possibly survive a Chicago winter in that shack?

But there's a flip side to that coin. Never allow yourself —or anyone who negotiates for you—unlimited authority. Some famous last words are, "Whatever you do is okay with me . . . you have total authority." You may recall that Neville Chamberlain went to Munich to negotiate with Hitler with unlimited authority. Certainly, he did not fare well as a negotiator.

If you extend authorization to others, always get them involved in setting an objective that they believe is attainable. They must feel committed to what you expect them to accomplish. Your negotiators are not errand boys or girls but responsible people who should have authority, but only up to a point. Ultimately say to them, "Go out there and try to get it for that amount. If you can, that's great. If you can't, come back and we'll discuss it further."

Earlier I mentioned that the worst person you can negotiate for is yourself. You are too emotionally involved, and it's all too easy to lose perspective. In addition, when you handle your own negotiations you have total authority, and it's easy to make snap decisions without making proper use of your time.

How can you get around this? By imposing checks and balances on yourself. By deliberately limiting yourself, at least for a period of time. By vowing, before you negotiate or interact, the equivalent of, "I'm going to pay no more than $1,200 for that TV console. That's it—not one cent more. If I can't get it for that price today, I'm going home." In other words, by being obedient to your own dictates.

If having too much authority is a handicap in negotiations, it follows that the worst person to negotiate for any organization is the chief executive officer. It is a truism that the worst person to negotiate for a city is the mayor, the worst for a state, the governor, and the worst for the United States, the president. The particular individual may be brilliant, patient, and expert but has too much authority.

There's another aspect of the Soviet approach I'd like to touch on: the use of emotions that seemingly aren't house-broken.

3. Emotional tactics

For years, Soviets have swept papers aside and lumbered out of meetings without provocation. They may even act personally offensive, all in the interest of provoking, distracting, or intimidating their opponents. Who can forget Nikita Khrushchev's pounding his shoe on a table at a session of the

United Nations? When people learned of that, their shocked reaction was, "My God! The man's a barbarian. He desecrated a world body with that kind of behavior. If my child did that, I'd call it a temper tantrum. Why, if he awakens one morning with heartburn, he's liable to blow up the world!"

Months later, someone enlarged the photo of Khrushchev pounding his shoe, then studied it with a magnifying glass. To his astonishment, there, under the table, were two other shoes, on the Soviet leader's feet. Now what does that mean? As I see it there are three possibilities:

1. The man has three feet. This alternative would appear somewhat remote.
2. That morning as he was getting dressed, he turned to Gromyko and said, "Comrade, pack the shoe in the brown paper bag. We'll use it at 3:00 P.M."
3. During the session he called to Commissar Ivanovich, "Pass down your shoe—we'll need it in a few minutes."

What we are talking about is a craftily planned, premeditated act designed to bring about a particular response. Was that calculated outburst effective? Probably so. People feel uneasy when confronted by irrationality joined at the hip with strength. They may even be inclined to give in to threats, to avoid getting hurt. It reminds one of the classic joke: Where can a 400-pound gorilla sleep? Anywhere it wants to. That may have been the reaction that the Soviet Union wanted.

Of course, one needn't pound on a table to be emotional. Even a common display of feelings can be used to manipulate. Have you ever tried to negotiate with someone who breaks down and cries? It's devastating. Think of your own experience in this regard. You've got all the facts and logic on your side as you deal with a spouse, parent, or child. Since your evidence is overwhelming, you've got them backed into a corner with no place to go. Suddenly tears well up in their eyes and begin to trickle down their cheeks.

How do you react? Do you think, "Okay, I got 'em—I'll move in for the kill"?

The hell you do. If you are like most of us, you back off and say, "Gee, I'm sorry I made you cry. I guess I came on a little strong." You probably go even further, "Not only will I give you what you originally wanted, but I'll throw in compensatory damages for making you cry. Here, take my charge card, go into town, and buy yourself something!"

Obviously, I'm not referring only to females crying. My personal opinion is that men's tears are more effective than women's. I say this because I'm aware of a company that's been trying to fire a big, husky male foreman for more than twelve months. The style of this outfit is to be very discreet. It does not hand out pink slips or ever call someone in and announce, "You're fired!"

Instead, it sets up a counseling session where the personnel manager chats with the employee to be discharged about "a life beyond the company's walls" and other career options. Usually, the employee responds to these subtle hints, leaves on his own, and even saves the company severance pay.

Here's the catch: In the past year this personnel manager has met with that foreman four times. On each occasion he has attempted to cue him that his services are no longer desired. Before they even get to the possible alternatives, the big male foreman has begun to sob and wail convulsively. This may be an artful acting job, but it unnerves the personnel manager, who afterward always mumbles to a peer, "Look—if *you* want to fire him, go to it. I can't!" Recently I learned that the outfit has given up on these exit interviews of the foreman. As far as I can tell, he's home free.

If tears are effective, whether spontaneous or staged, so is anger.

Here's a hypothetical situation: You and I are negotiating. We spent the morning in your office discussing a software program for my company's computers. You're anxious to sell me your services. Just as we are about to discuss cost, you glance at your watch and say, "Why don't we break for lunch? There's a swanky place around the corner where they know me, so we won't need a reservation."

Ushered to your usual table, we glance at expensive entrées on the menu, then order drinks and food. Sipping my martini, I ask you, "Tell me—what were you thinking of charging for this software program?"

You answer, "Well, to be frank with you, Herb, I was thinking about $240,000."

I explode. I become apoplectic. Raising my voice, I exclaim, "What are you trying to pull? Are you *crazy?* An astronomical $240,000? What do you think I am?"

Embarrassed, since everyone's staring at us, you cover your lips and murmur, "Shhhh!"

I raise my voice another decibel. "You really must be out of your *mind!* That's highway *robbery!*"

You now feel like crawling under the table, for many diners in the establishment know you, though they don't know me. The maitre d' is staring at you not knowing what to do. Even our waiter with the flaming shashlik sword hesitates to approach us. He's afraid he might get hurt. You know in your gut that onlookers are asking themselves, "What did he say to provoke that guy? Was he trying to cheat him?" I've publicly intimidated you Soviet-style, with feigned outrage. Should you ever talk to me again, it is not likely to be in a public place. But if you do, it is fairly certain you will expect to get much less than the $240,000.

Oddly enough, *silence*, which is much easier to carry out, can be just as effective as tears, anger, and aggression.

Of all these emotional ploys this is the one that has the greatest impact on me. My wife and I have been happily married for twenty-two years, but when we have a dispute her top tactic is always silence—withdrawal or, as I call it, abstinence. You must understand my vulnerability because I am away from home so much. Assume that I return from a two-week trip overseas, craving love and affection. Anxiously,

I enter my house. "Hello, hello, I'm home, honey! Where is everybody?"

Silence.

After waiting for a response, I try again. "Hey, it's me. I'm here. Anybody home?"

Silence.

Finally, after what seems like an interminable delay, my wife appears. She seems very reserved and indifferent to my arrival. Nevertheless, I rush up to her and announce, "Honey, it's me! I'm home!"

Silence.

"What's the matter honey? Anybody sick? Anybody die? What's wrong?"

Silence.

Her face is expressionless and she's looking right through me. What am I thinking? "Oh oh, she knows something I don't know. I know what I'll do. I'll confess." Now what if I confess to the wrong thing? I'll go from one problem to two problems very quickly.

When you give someone the silent treatment you often force the other person to talk, if only out of discomfort. They inadvertently give you information you might otherwise not receive. Consequently, there is a favorable shift in the balance of power.

There are many other emotional tactics that are often in evidence. *Laughter* is one. If you decide not to discuss anything seriously; if you choose to change the subject; or if you elect to put someone down, a burst of derisive laughter is as devastating as the swish of a samurai sword.

Supposing you are holding a garage sale and I stop by on a weekend to examine your merchandise. You have an old sled upon which there is a handwritten piece of paper that says, "Rare antique—make an offer." Since *Citizen Kane* was my all-time favorite movie, I want to make this "Rosebud" mine. As you approach I blurt out, "I'll give you $7 for the sled."

For some reason unknown to me, you suddenly burst out laughing. What am I thinking? "What's so funny? . . . Maybe the zipper on my pants is open? . . . Gee, I didn't mean to start so low for a genuine rare antique!" One would have to be very secure about their appearance and knowledge of old sleds not to raise their offer if they really wanted this object.

Walking out is another emotional gambit. Especially if it's unexpected, a precipitous withdrawal may startle and embarrass the side left behind. It raises additional issues and problems and creates uncertainty about the future.

Imagine this situation: A husband and wife meet after work at a quiet restaurant for dinner. Halfway through the meal she informs him of a wonderful promotion, with a 50 percent salary increase, that has been offered her if she relocates to a different part of the country. From his expression, it is apparent that he does not share her pride and excitement.

He remarks, "But what about me and my job?"

She responds, "Don't worry—you can come with me. As for that job, you can equal it *anywhere!*"

Suddenly, without warning, he curtly says, "Excuse me." He stands up and walks toward the door.

Five minutes after the unexpected departure, amidst her conflicting feelings, she is thinking about what happened and evaluating her current situation:

Did he leave because he was upset?

Is he all right?

Maybe he only went to put money in the parking meter.

Perhaps he's in the rest room or making a phone call.

Did I say anything to hurt him?

Is he depressed or just envious?

Do I have sufficient cash to pay the bill?

Did he have an accident?

Has he left me for good?

Is he coming back?

How will I get home?

To further increase her anxiety, the waiter asks, "Should I

serve both entrées now or hold them under the keep-hot lights until your friend returns?"

Speaking of raising anxiety, the *veiled threat* is a potent weapon. It makes use of the other side's imagination because what they think *might* happen is always more frightening than what *could* happen. You see, if an opponent believes someone has the capacity to execute a threat, the threat perceived is more fearsome than the threat enacted.

For instance, if I were involved in an adversary negotiation with you and wanted to elevate your stress level, I would adroitly use ambiguities and generalities. I'd never say the equivalent of "I'll fracture your right index finger!" That's not only too specific, but it's downright boorish. Instead, I'd look you right in the eye and say, "I *never* forget a face, and I *always* pay my debts!" Who knows what that even means? Yet if you thought I had the capacity and determination and was crazy enough, it might affect your composure.

Of course, a shrewd Soviet will rarely carry out a threat—only enough to keep his power credible; because once the threat is enacted, the stress is reduced and the other side adjusts and copes.

In 1979, there was the possibility of a police strike in New Orleans that might cause the annual Mardi Gras to be canceled. As long as this was a credible threat, the union organizers had maximum power in negotiating with the city for recognition.

Once they made the mistake of actually going on strike and causing the Mardi Gras to be curtailed and public opinion to shift against them, they lost all bargaining leverage. The upshot was that the teamsters' attempt to organize a police union was thwarted.

Several years ago I went to Ravinia, a music festival held each summer in a suburb north of Chicago. Since close parking is always a problem, I was elated to find a space on a quiet private road not too far from the event. As I got out of my auto I noticed that the car directly behind me had what looked like an advertising circular on the windshield. Being inquisitive, I stopped to read it, and I reprint its contents below:

> This vehicle is parked on private property. The make, model and license number have been recorded. If this improper parking is repeated a second time this vehicle will be towed to Klempner Brothers where the interior will be removed by fire and the auto will be compressed into a scrap cube approximately $1\frac{1}{2}' \times 3'$. The cube will be shipped (freight collect) to your home for use as a coffee table and to serve as a constant reminder not to park on private property.

Undoubtedly, this was some sort of joke. But not knowing the stability of the author, and needing a car more than a coffee table, I decided to find another parking space.

Although there are a great many other emotional tactics, it is fitting to close this representative sampling with one that should sound familiar. Listen to the following telephone conversation between a mother and her mature and independent offspring.

MOTHER: Hello, Pat! Do you know who this is? It's your—

PAT: Gee, Mom, how are you? I've been meaning to call.

MOTHER: It's okay—you don't have to call me. I'm *only* your mother. Why should you have to spend a dime?

PAT: Aw, Mom, c'mon. I've been very busy at work. How do you feel?

MOTHER: How does a person my age feel? Listen, I am celebrating your twenty-ninth birthday this Saturday night and have invited my best friends from the club to meet you. I've ordered a beautiful cake and bought your favorite food, so . . .

PAT: But moth-er, I intended to go away this weekend. I told you about—

MOTHER: You mean you can't find a few hours on your busy schedule for me?

PAT: No, it's not that. It's just that I've planned this trip and
    have made—
MOTHER: All right, Pat, I understand. I'm sorry to bother you.
    I'll just tell my friends that you are too busy for me.
PAT: *Please*, Mom—I'm not saying that.
MOTHER: No, I understand. Don't concern yourself about
    me. I'll manage somehow. After all, no law says a child
    has to see his mother.

Maybe this sketch is somewhat melodramatic, but the tactic
is easily recognizable as *giving guilt*. In *The Two-Thousand-
Year-Old Man*, Mel Brooks does a great caricature of the use
of guilt. He has a mother and father trudge through the rain
to visit their son's cave. Upon arrival, they are warmly
greeted and invited inside. But they meekly stand outside,
saying, "It's okay. It's good enough for us to stand in the rain.
We don't mind."

The bestowal of guilt occurs in close relationships, but
it also is used beyond the circle of friends and family. Have
you ever asked your boss for a raise and heard him respond,
"You think you've got a complaint, let me tell you about the
cross I have to bear"? Whatever the injustice of your case, his
grievances with top management make yours pale by com-
parison. You have just been one-upped. When you leave
the martyr's presence you feel selfish for even bothering him
with your petty complaint.

Why do people use these emotional maneuvers? *Because
they work!* They succeed if we don't recognize what's really
happening. We say to ourselves, "Oh, that's just the way he
or she is. They can't help it." As if they were born with a
manipulative chromosome. Certainly most people do not plan
to stage these ploys. They unconsciously revert to successful
proven techniques to maintain the upper hand. Yet there are
some who use compassion and guilt as part of their regular
repertoire.

I once heard about an office products salesman who perfected an emotional tactic to a virtual science. When making his sales calls he kept a running stop watch in the left pocket of his shirt, under his suit jacket. This congenial seller spoke virtually nonstop from the time he got in the door. When he sensed he was losing the potential sale, he would stand up and approach the customer, ostensibly to say goodbye. Looking downcast and depressed he would pause during a prolonged handshake.

Because of their close proximity and the prevailing silence, the prospective customer could now hear a slight clicking sound, "Tic-tic-tic-tic." Hearing the ticking, the customer would usually say, "What's that noise?"

After pretending surprise, the seller would tap his heart and say, "Oh, it's only my pacemaker. By the way, might I disturb you for a glass of water?" From what I heard, he always got the water and usually made the sale thereafter. The person who told me this story was one of the victims of this tactic. As he put it, "It was a hole puncher, a stapler, and a calculator later before I realized that pacemakers don't make noise."

Most of us would question this behavior on ethical grounds. I present it not to be copied or condoned, but to be understood. Yet when the guilt tactic is modified to eliminate the obvious lie and is used in the service of high ideals, it is often applauded.

Mahatma Gandhi is generally revered as a practitioner of nonviolence, but his tactical means were just a variation of the old guilt ploy. What this emaciated ascetic was really saying to Great Britain was, "If you don't give independence to India, I'm going on a public hunger strike. Each day I will deteriorate further, and the blame for my death will be upon your soul." His ends may have been lofty, but the means are just the good old-fashioned guilt-giving tactics. They ultimately worked, stirring the world conscience and forcing England to change her colonial policy.

Why have I elaborated so much on these Soviet-style emo-

tional tactics? *Not* because I want you to use them, but
because I want you to recognize them, so you won't be hood-
winked. A familiarity and understanding of even the most
shady means will not corrupt you. Mere knowledge of evil
does not constitute sin. In order to have sin you need knowledge, plus motive, plus *action*. Unmistakably, I am advocating
recognition and not adoption.

Remember that a tactic that is identified for what it is—
a tactic that's seen through—is ineffective. Your opponent
may have a handgun, but it is now without cartridges. In brief,
a tactic perceived is no tactic!

For instance, let's backtrack to the "nibble." Supposing I
went through my entire routine in a men's store. After setting
it up beautifully and trying on the suit, I proclaim, "How
about throwing in a tie free!"

What happens if the salesman diagnoses the maneuver? He
may begin to chortle and amidst peals of laughter say to me,
"That was a magnificent nibble. I love the way you set it up.
Please, it's not fair to keep this to myself. We've got to share it
with others." At this point he calls out to his fellow salesmen, "Hey, Arnold, Larry, and Irv—come here, will you? I
want you to hear a fantastic nibble! It's a scream." Turning
back to me and still laughing, he exclaims, "You've got to do
it for them . . . *from the beginning*—they'll love it!"

How do you think even I would react to all this commotion?
Flustered and embarrassed, I'd probably mumble, "Aw, I was
just horsing around. Give me two suits—full price, of course!"

Let's stay with the nibble for another moment. Assume that
you are a salesperson in an establishment, or anyone who has
invested heavily in a transaction, and someone tries to pull the
nibble on you. There are three simple counters that can be
used to out-thrust and out-parry such a person:

1. *No authority*. Make it clear that you would like to
   help but lack the authority to grant the request. Say,
   "I'm sorry. The last person who did such a thing was

fired and is now a homesteader in the South Bronx."

2. *Legitimacy.* Post a sign on the wall that states in effect, WITH THIS SALE THERE WILL BE NO EMBELLISHMENTS.

3. *Knowingly laugh.* Using a light touch, acknowledge the tactic and praise the customer's skill in carrying it out so well. You are chuckling with the customer, *not* laughing at him.

Speaking of counteracting emotional tactics, this brings me to a question that I have often been asked lately. The questioner is commonly a woman executive in business or government. The problem generally develops in meetings with peers and higher-ups. Apparently, while this female manager is stating her opinion or rendering a report, a male staff member will habitually engage in table thumping or verbal bullying by raising his voice or even shouting. The advice being solicited is, "How do you deal with this *verbal bully* engaged in tactical intimidation?"

Fundamentally, it is important to realize that the so-called intimidator or "man child" is the person with the problem. Despite the provocation, the recipient of this abuse must remain calm and serene. Never try to slug it out with the bully, but don't back down either. Continue to state your reasoned ideas with confidence. If he continues, lower your voice below its normal pitch. Should his rantings persist, you may not even be heard, but your control will be in stark contrast to his infantile behavior. By this time those present will identify with you and the verbal bully will be an embarrassment and no longer an amusement.

The verbal bully and those who practice these emotional ploys have usually learned this behavior as children. It may have been observed in a role model or picked up through trial and error. Those tactics which led to rewards were retained, and those which resulted in punishment or pain were discarded.

Not long ago, I overheard a child in a department store say to his parent, "If I don't get a toy, I'll lie down on the escalator!" Five minutes later, the youngster walked past me with a toy under one arm and a self-satisfied smile on his face. Should such a child be continually rewarded for threats and temper tantrums, these tactics will become ingrained in the child's approach to controlling others.

Be reminded that when an adult negotiator occasionally lets fly—engages in a verbal attack—it can be assumed that it is usually unconscious behavior. The best track under these circumstances is to wait until the outburst is over and then thank the person for explaining his or her views so clearly and forcefully.

This reaction on your part most always makes the other person regret the outburst, and the person may even become more amenable.

Since the remaining three steps in the competitive Soviet style are consistent with what has been said previously, we can now pick up the pace.

4. Adversary concessions viewed as weakness

The Russians, going back to the czars, have always respected power while exhibiting distrust for foreigners that occasionally bordered on paranoia. They still believe that the best way of gaining the cooperation of others is to exhibit a willingness to employ overwhelming force. In this, their philosophy of détente resembles that of the Roman Empire, which maintained peace (Pax Romana) based on a frequently demonstrated readiness to use force.

Whereas western diplomats generally regard negotiations as compromise between conflicting positions, the Kremlin sees them as a struggle to be won. To them it is a figurative street fight, and if an opponent adheres to the Marquis of Queensbury Rules they begin to question the opposition's real strength.

Obviously the same attitude of victory at all costs does not pervade our thinking. Sure, there are some parts of our society where strong competitive attitudes prevail: presidential elections, competitive sports, litigation in our adversary legal system, and business, where we sometimes speak of "winning a promotion" and "beating the competition."

Conceivably, our own home-grown Soviets, who believe that ruthless competition is part of the divine plan, have generalized from limited observations of these areas. In spite of this Win-Lose minority, most of us tend to accept a solution that is best for all rather than trying to get our own way. Moreover, we may mistakenly ascribe the same motives and philosophy to *all others* with whom we deal.

This means that the typical American or western negotiator, when confronted with a stalemate, is often willing to make the first concession to get things moving. We assume that the other party will respect this candor and collaborative spirit and reciprocate. Actually, if you are dealing with a Soviet-style operator, the opposite is true.

During the armistice negotiation ending the Korean War, both sides stated their initial demands regarding the location of the final truce line. Obviously, they were far apart. Suddenly the United Nations negotiators, departing from appropriate adversary bargaining practices, made a quick major concession. In trying to be conciliatory with the "Soviets" from North Korea, we actually revealed our final fallback position. Instead of this being perceived as reasonableness, it gave the impression of weakness to our opponents and hardened their negotiating posture.

The American admiral, C. Turner Joy, who headed the U.N. negotiating team at Panmunjom, later admitted that this quick concession (which was never returned in kind) gave the Communists a big advantage in the negotiations. Writing of this experience he said, "Because of our American tendency to feel that a deadlocked issue should be solved by mutual concessions, the Communists are on favorable ground in applying their delaying tactics." In essence, when dealing with Soviets, whatever their pedigree, should you generously concede something to them, it is unlikely that a reciprocal concession will be forthcoming.

Remember the example of the Soviets' trying to purchase property on the North Shore of Long Island? We saw how they offered $125,000 against an asking price of $420,000. When after three months the sellers reduced their demand to $360,000, how did they respond? Before answering that question, I ask you, "What would most of us do if we were in their position as buyers?"

If our attitude is embodied in the sayings "Give a little, get a little," or "One hand washes the other," we would make a counter-offer increasing the initial lowball offer.

The Soviet Union's negotiators, like the North Koreans, did no such thing. On the contrary, they remained firm at $125,000. They viewed the $60,000 concession by the sellers not as a gracious gesture, but as vindication and a sign of weakness. As a consequence, they held firm at their initial offer for eight months; then they penny-pinched their way to $133,000.

It should not have been unexpected, as the next step in their tactical pattern indicates.

5. Stingy in concessions

At the outset we must realize that the Soviets, because of their system, have two built-in negotiating advantages in dealing with the United States:

1. *More information.* Because of the closed nature of their society, contrasted with our freedom, they always start out knowing more about our real needs, priorities, and deadlines than we know about theirs. Their representatives and agents watch our media, read our newspapers, and even subscribe to our scientific publi-

cations. Essentially what we know about them is what
the Politburo wants to tell us.

2. *More time.* In the main, very little turnover occurs
in the top-echelon Kremlin leadership. Whether it's
Khrushchev, Brezhnev, or Gromyko, their tenure
seems endless. By contrast, the United States has regular leadership changes due to shorter political cycles.
Further compounding our inability to use time effectively, are the incessant popularity polls and the
dynamic nature of our society, which causes personnel
changes and a compelling need to produce quick
tangible results.

As Secretary of State Dean Acheson said more than thirty
years ago, "The business of dealing with the Russians is a long,
long job." The nature of their system, with its state-controlled
media and absence of accountability, gives them the luxury of
patience.

With this advantage they can establish longer time frames
to get what they want. During this period they attempt to
wear us down through endless delays, issuing constant *"nyets"*
and making meager concessions, separated by long intervals.

To most Americans, "Time is money," and this attitude
has conditioned us to observe and respect schedules and deadlines. As a correlative to this attitude, we have been taught to
revere efficiency, which means we prefer meetings and negotiations that are crisp and brief.

More than one hundred years ago Alexis de Tocqueville
said of the American character: "There is a tendency to
abandon mature design to gratify a momentary passion."

One of the most decisive determinants in the outcome of
any negotiation is the size and number of concessions made by
one side compared to those of its adversary. Slick Soviet-style
negotiators, wherever reared, will always try to induce you
to make the first concession. Thereafter, they will try to avoid
any reciprocation. When you yield something to them, what

you receive in return will be of lesser value by comparision. By practicing forebearance, competitive negotiators strive to see that the size and number of times you concede is greater than theirs.

6. Ignore deadlines

Throughout this discourse on the competitive Win-Lose negotiating style, I have been using the practices of the Soviet Union as our model. Without doubt, their key tactical element, serving as the fulcrum around which the other parts revolve, is *time*.

As we have seen, whenever you negotiate with a Soviet you must be patient. Everything will start on time, but the delays will seem endless. If you attempt to speed things along, your request will be discussed and debated, but nothing will change. Even when arriving at the end they are not in a hurry, for they know that all deadlines are the product of a negotiation. Therefore, it's negotiable! They will try to convince you that the original deadline is for real, but they have never been persuaded.

Coming back to the purchase of property on Long Island's North Shore, when we left off it was four months prior to the expiration of the option. The Soviets had just offered $133,000 against an asking price of $360,000. From then on, little occurred until the flurry of the following Russian moves (at the left is when their offer was made relative to the deadline, and on the right the amount):

twenty days prior	$145,000
five days prior	164,000
three days prior	176,000
one day prior	182,000
Deadline Day	197,000

From these figures it is evident that virtually all the Soviet activity was compressed into the last five days prior to the deadline. When the deadline passed, it looked as though both sides were hopelessly deadlocked. They were still a considerable distance apart: Soviet offer $197,000 versus sellers' asking price of $360,000.

The real estate agent was about to put this large land parcel back on the market, when he was contacted by the Soviets, one day after the option had expired. After another week of frenetic negotiations, the Soviets paid $216,000 in cash to the owner, who needed the money desperately because of a "liquidity problem."

Needless to say, the final sale price doesn't always tell the whole story, but there is considerable evidence that the Soviet purchase price was way below the market price. This negotiation vignette dramatically depicts the Soviet style in action.

The aftermath is also interesting. The Soviets now had their property, which required rezoning before it could be used for their purposes. In going before the requisite board they encountered the former owner, who was still seething.

After submitting many sets of revised plans and after inordinate delays, the Soviets realized they would not be able to secure approval for the needed changes. Almost a year from the date of the original purchase, they resold the acreage for $372,000. Subsequently, with toned down negotiating tactics, they acquired suitable land in King's Point, Long Island, not far from the old Guggenheim estate.

Once again, I have presented the Soviet competitive style in great detail *not* because I want you to operate this way. As I said before, I would like you to recognize these tactics so you will not be victimized by them. To further reiterate, *a tactic perceived is no tactic.*

For Soviet tactics to work, all three of these criteria must exist:

1. *No continuing relationship.* The negotiation must be a *one-shot transaction* where the perpetrator is sure he

will not need his victim again. Consequently, if your relationship is a continuing one, you may win a pyrrhic victory at the expense of mortgaging your future relationship.

Let's say, for example, that I, as a Soviet negotiator, "sting" you and get away scot free. Will you realize that you've been duped? Maybe not instantly, but eventually you will become aware of what happened. Should you manage to ignore the blood on your shoes, someone will tap you on the shoulder and politely say, "Pardon me, but there's a metallic object protruding from your back, and . . . oh, yes—you are bleeding profusely." Even the slowest learner will realize what occurred.

No matter how upset you may be, you have little recourse. However, should we see each other again, you could be waiting for me. Supposing I still have more power than you in this second encounter, your attitude might be, "I'm going down again, but he's going down with me. I'll pull the temple down on both our heads."

In essence, you're now willing to sacrifice yourself if it means getting back at me. What you have done is adopted the *Lose-Lose strategy* embodied in the expression "We'll all bleed together."

2. *No remorse afterward.* Whether it's derived from ethics, morality, or religious upbringing, most of us have a concept of what constitutes fair play. You and your conscience must go on living with the tactical means used to achieve this victory. If afterward, you are overcome by a sense of guilt and contrition, was winning this way worthwhile? As the late Janis Joplin said, "Don't compromise yourself, because it's all you've got!"

Nevertheless, those who believe that the end justifies the means have no difficulty with this criterion.

3. *No awareness by victim.* The potential victim must be naïve—innocent and unaware—at least momentarily. If the prey understands the hunting game, they are unlikely to remain in the line of fire. Therefore, regardless of the skill of the hunter, the cooperation of an unsuspecting mark is required.

For this reason alone, it is advisable to recognize the competitive Win-Lose style. If enough people had this knowledge, we would be able to deny the slick Soviets among us their cheap victories at the expense of the unsuspecting. In fact, if this knowledge were widespread, we would neutralize competitive tactics and minimize game playing.

All right, let's discuss you, the reader. How can you protect yourself so you don't get a stiletto in your back? How can you guard against having blood trickling down your leg? The answer is the ability to anticipate and recognize this style.

Remember, the Soviet's first criterion for springing the trap is a one-shot deal. So when your old jalopy conks out and you rush to see a used-car dealer in downtown New York City, Los Angeles, or Philadelphia, what kind of tactics are you likely to encounter? Contrast this to a new-car dealer in Billings, Montana, or Rhinelander, Wisconsin, where reputation is needed for repeat business and survival.

Wherever you may be, should the behavior of the other party cause your antennas to quiver "Win-Lose," you have three options:

1. You always have other alternatives, so pivot on your heels and walk away. Since life is so short, you may even want to tell the manipulator to negotiate with himself or herself.

2. If you have the time and inclination you can enter the fray. By your counter-moves you may well beat the devil at his own game.

3. Artfully switch the relationship from a competitive Win-Lose contest to a collaborative encounter in which you can both meet your needs.

In the next chapters I'll show you why and how this transformation can take place, and I will explain negotiations in which both sides can win.

*Money talks . . . but
does it tell the truth?*

8. Negotiating for mutual satisfaction

There is a legendary story that has become part of the folklore of negotiations:

A brother and sister have been squabbling over some leftover pie, with each insisting on the larger slice. Each wants to get a big piece and not be cheated by the sibling. Just as the boy has gained control of the knife and is poised to hack off the lion's share for himself, the mother or father arrives on the scene.

In the tradition of King Solomon, the parent says, "Hold it! I don't care who cuts that pie into two pieces, but whoever does has to give the *other* the right to select the piece they want." Naturally, to protect himself, the boy cuts the slab into two pieces of equal size.

The tale may be apocryphal, but its underlying moral has continuing revelance today. There are many situations in which the needs of the protagonists are not really in opposition. If the focus shifts from defeating each other to defeating the problem, everyone can benefit.

In a collaborative Win-Win negotiation we are trying to produce an outcome that provides acceptable gain to all parties. Conflict is regarded as a natural part of the human condition. If conflict is viewed as a problem to be solved, creative solutions can be found that enhance the positions of both sides, and the parties may even be brought closer together.

It may be a coincidence, but in collective bargaining between management and labor the metaphor of the pie is customarily bandied about. One side will often say, "We just want our share of the pie!" However, if the pie is seen as a fixed sum of money, what one side gains the other side must necessarily lose. Consider the following:

After a bargaining impasse, a union goes on strike. If the union wins, the wages lost during the strike will exceed the benefits gained. Conversely, with the strike, management will lose more than the cost of granting the demands without the strike. So both lose with the strike. If there were no strike, in a climate of trust they could achieve a settlement that would enable both sides to get what they want.

In spite of this logic, we continue to witness strikes where not only do union and management lose, but the public, the economy, and even the national interest suffer. Why does this happen? Perhaps part of the problem is the analogy of the pie. When we converge on a fixed sum and start to argue back and forth making demands, counter-demands, conclusions, and ultimatums, there is no likelihood of a creative outcome. Instead, we should see our true interests as complementary and in effect ask each other, "How can we get together in a way that will make the total pie bigger, so there's more to go around?"

Obviously, this does not refer to labor relations alone, but to each and every negotiation where relationships are ongoing. If you think for a moment, you'll see that covers nearly all your negotiations.

Since nature does not create all human beings alike, your needs and my needs are usually not identical. Therefore, it's possible for both of us to emerge victorious.

The uniqueness of each person seems to be an accepted fact—at least on an intellectual level. Then why do we approach most negotiations as if they were adversary encounters, where your satisfaction must be at the expense of the other side? The reason is that in most negotiations, discussion is about a "fixed sum," usually money.

Why is negotiation talk always about money, or a form thereof, like price, rate, salary, or "bread-and-butter issues"? Why is everyone seemingly hung up on money? It's not the money—it's the m-o-n-e-y! Because m-o-n-e-y is specific, precise, and quantifiable. It gives feedback on whether your other needs are being met. *It helps you keep score.* It's a way of measuring progress. It's a yardstick for determining worth, as some homemakers know all too well. It's even a means of encoding distasteful messages.

What if I go in to my boss and say, "To work for a jerk like you, under these degrading circumstances, I want more money!" Such candor is unlikely to endear me to my superior. Therefore, I've learned to convert into code my real feelings and frustrations and simply say, "I'd like to make more money."

Not only is this pure monetary message more palatable, but the boss puts his arm around my shoulder and exclaims, "I like ambitious people. You and I, we'll go to the top together."

Many of us have been conditioned from the time we were youngsters to accept money as a conversational topic. Some have been led to believe that their favorite color should be green—dollar green. Listen to people talk and you sometimes think that they are living dollar signs. But if you believe that most negotiations pivot on money alone, you're mistaken. People are not the way they speak or appear to be. Surely money *is* a need, but it's merely one of many. If you neglect their other needs, satisfying people's dollar need alone will *not* make them happy. Let me prove this via a hypothetical situation:

While thumbing through a magazine one evening, two people living together—say a husband and wife—notice an antique clock used as a background piece in an advertisement.

The wife comments, "Isn't that the most beautiful clock you ever saw? Wouldn't it look wonderful in our center entrance hallway or foyer?"

The husband replies, "It sure would! I wonder what it costs. There's no price tag in the ad."

Together they decide to look for the clock in antique shops. They mutually agree that should they find it, they'll pay no more than $500.

After three months of searching, they finally see the clock displayed at an antique-show booth. "There it is!" the wife exclaims excitedly.

"You're right, that's it!" says the husband. "Remember," he adds, "we aren't going to pay more than $500!"

They approach the booth. "Oh-oh," mutters the wife. "There's a sign on top of the clock that says $750. We might as well go home. We said we'd spend no more than $500, remember?"

"I remember," says the husband, "but let's take a stab at it anyway. We've been looking for so long." They huddle privately and appoint him the negotiator, with an outside chance to secure it for the $500.

Gathering his courage, he addresses himself to the clock salesman. "I notice you have a *small* clock for sale. I notice the alleged price on top. I also notice a little dust around the sign giving it an antique quality." Building momentum, the husband now says, "Tell you what I'll do. I'll make you one offer and one offer alone for the clock, and that'll be it. And I'm sure it'll thrill your very being. Are you ready?" He pauses for effect. "Well here it is—$250."

The clock salesman, without batting an eye, says, "It's yours. Sold."

What's the husband's first reaction? Elation? Is he saying to himself, "I did exceedingly well, beating my objective by a considerable amount"? Heck no! You know as well as I do, because we've all been in similar situations, his initial reaction is, "How stupid of me! I should have offered the guy $150!" You also know his second reaction: "There must be something wrong with the clock!"

As the husband carries the clock to his car, he says to himself, "This sure is light, because I'm not *that* strong! I'll bet some internal pieces are missing!"

Nevertheless, he puts it in the entrance hallway of their home. It *looks* stunning. It seems to be working fine, but he and his wife feel uneasy.

After they retire, they get up three times in the middle of the night. Why? They're sure they didn't hear the clock chime. This goes on for days and sleepless nights. Their health is deteriorating rapidly, and they are becoming hypertensive. Why? Because the clock salesman had the effrontery to sell them that clock for $250.

If he'd been a decent, reasonable, compassionate person, he'd have permitted them the pleasure and self-satisfaction of bargaining up to $497. By saving them $247, he'll eventually cost them three times that amount in irritation bills. The classic mistake in this negotiation was that all attention was directed to a single facet—the price. If the couple were one-dimensional, having only a money need, they would have been ecstatic. However, like all of us, they are multi-faceted, having many needs, some unconscious and unacknowledged.

Satisfying this couple's price demand alone did not make them happy. Apparently getting the clock at their desired price wasn't enough. For them, under these circumstances, the negotiation ended too quickly. They needed a little chitchat, a discussion to establish trust, and even some bargaining. If the husband had been able to pit his wits successfully against the seller, this process would have made him feel better—about the purchase and about himself.

Previously, we said that negotiation is an activity in which parties are trying to satisfy their needs. Yet their real needs are seldom what they seem to be, because the negotiators try to conceal them or don't recognize them. Consequently, negotiations are never totally for what is being openly talked about or contested, be it price, services, products, territory, concessions, interest rates, or money. What is being discussed, and the *manner in which it is being considered*, are used to satisfy psychological needs.

A negotiation is more than an exchange of material objects. It is a *way* of acting and behaving that can develop understanding, belief, acceptance, respect, and trust. It is the manner of your approach, the tone of your voice, the attitude you convey, the methods you use, and the concern you exhibit for the other side's feelings and needs.

All these things comprise the *process* of negotiation. Hence, the way you go about trying to obtain your objective may in and of itself meet some of the other party's needs.

Up to this point we have explored why negotiations often get unnecessarily bogged down in adversary struggles, conflicts that may not benefit either side. If negotiation involves the satisfaction of needs, we have suggested that the process itself—the way we go about resolving the conflict—may meet the needs of the participants. Further, since all people are unique, the needs of prospective opponents can be harmonized or reconciled.

Let me now elaborate on how the negotiating process and reconciling opponent's needs can be used to bring about collaborative Win-Win outcomes:

1. Using the process to meet needs

At the outset of a negotiation you should always come on like velvet, not coarse sandpaper. State your case moderately, scratch your head, and admit you might even be in error. Remember, "To err is human; to forgive, divine." Don't hesitate to say, "I need your help with this problem, 'cause I dunno."

Always address the other side with tact and concern for their dignity. Even if they have a reputation for being obnoxious, negative, and contrary, they will be disarmed by an approach that conveys positive expectations. If given a chance, most people try to be accommodating and play the role suggested for them. In other words, people tend to behave the way you expect them to behave.

Try to see the problem from *their point of view* or frame of reference. Listen with empathy, which means stop yourself from working on counter arguments while they're speaking. Don't ever be abrasive, because *how* you say something will often determine the response you get. Avoid using absolutes in responding to them. Learn to preface your replies with "What I think I may have heard you say . . ."

This *"lubricant demeanor"* will soften your words, consecrate your actions, and minimize the friction. Follow these guidelines and you will acquire an ally as both of you search for a mutually acceptable solution.

Let me show how this approach worked in a brief encounter I had several years ago:

An associate and I were in Manhattan on business. Since we had some time before our first appointment that morning, we were having a leisurely breakfast. After ordering, my companion went outside for a newspaper. Five minutes later he returned empty-handed. He was shaking his head and mumbling expletives under his breath.

"What's the matter?" I asked.

He responded, "These damn people! I walked up to this newsstand across the street, and as I took a paper, I handed the guy a $10 bill. Instead of getting change, he pulled the paper right out from under my arm. There I was in a state of shock and he started lecturing me that he was not in the business of making change during the rush hour."

Concluding breakfast, we discussed the episode. My companion took the position that the arrogance was in the air and that his adversary was such an "ornery cuss" that he would never cash a $10 bill for anyone. Taking up the challenge, I crossed the street as my friend watched from outside the restaurant.

As the newsstand proprietor turned to me I said meekly, "Sir . . . excuse me . . . but I wonder if you could help me with a problem. I'm a stranger in town and I need a *New York Times.* I only have a $10 bill. What can I do?" Without hesitation, he handed me the paper and said, "Here, take it; get the change and come back!"

Exuding confidence, I triumphantly strode across the street with the "trophy" in my hand. My associate, who had observed what he later called "The Miracle on 54th Street," was shaking his head.

Casually, I remarked, "Score another one for the process. It's all in the approach!"

2. Harmonizing or reconciling needs

Unfortunately, when people see themselves as adversaries they deal at arm's length or even through third parties. From this distance they state demands and counter-demands, pronounce conclusions, and hurl ultimatums at each other. Since each party attempts to increase his relative power, significant data, facts, and information are hoarded. One's feelings, attitudes, and real needs are concealed lest they be used against one. Obviously in such a climate, it is virtually impossible to negotiate for the satisfaction of mutual needs.

However, with the realization that human beings are matchless, it follows that their goals cannot be mutually exclusive. In this climate, candor and trust can be established and there will be an exchange of attitudes, facts, personal feelings, and needs. With this free interaction and sharing, creative solutions may be found that make both sides winners.

For example, in the mid-1940s, the late Howard Hughes produced a motion picture, *The Outlaw*. It featured Jane Russell, a beautiful brunette with an impressive cleavage. The movie may have been forgettable, but the billboards advertising the film were memorable. There was Jane Russell lying on some hay, supine in the sky. As a youngster I can still remember getting up real high and trying to look down.

At the time, Hughes was so enamored of Russell that he signed her to a one-year, one-million-dollar personal-services contract.

Twelve months later, Jane said, in effect, "I'd like my money pursuant to the contract."

Howard claimed he wasn't "liquid" at that moment but had plenty of assets. The position of the actress was that she didn't want excuses; she wanted her money. Hughes kept on telling her about his temporary cash-flow problem and asking her to wait. Russell kept pointing to the legal contract, which clearly called for payment at year's end.

The demands of each side seemed irreconcilable. Acting as adversaries in the competitive mode, they were dealing through their attorneys. What was formerly a close working relationship had become a win-lose struggle. Rumors were rampant that the matter would end up in the legal system. (Keep in mind that Howard Hughes is the person who would subsequently spend $12 million in legal fees in the controversy over control of TWA.) If this conflict were litigated, who would win? Perhaps the only winners would be the lawyers!

How was this conflict resolved? In effect, Russell and Hughes wisely said, "Look, you and I are different people. We have different goals. Let's see if we can't share information, feelings, and needs in an atmosphere of trust." That's precisely what they did. Then, acting as collaborators, they came up with a creative solution to their problem that satisfied them both.

They transformed the original contract into a twenty-year deal for $50,000 per annum. The package contained the same amount of money, but it was now shaped differently. As a result, Hughes solved his "liquidity problem" and kept the interest on the principal sum. On the other hand, Russell benefited by spreading her taxable income over a period of years, probably decreasing her taxes. By receiving what amounted to an annuity for twenty years, she solved her day-to-day financial problems.

The acting profession ordinarily is not very secure. Moreover, she not only "saved face," but she won! Remember that when you're dealing with an eccentric like Howard Hughes, even if you're right you may not win. In terms of individual —and different—needs, Russell and Hughes were both big winners.

Conflict

Conflict is an unavoidable part of life. Some of us have goals that are in opposition. But conflict, no matter what its form—from the disposition of a slab of pie to the distribution of a million dollars—will often arise even if both sides are in agreement on what they want.

Here's an example where both parties want the same thing but the conflict is over how to get it (or the means):

Near the end of a football game, the home team has moved down the field, only two yards away from the goal line. During a time out the quarterback urges that they go for the touchdown. The coach is insistent that they try for a field goal. Both have the same goal—to win the game. The disagreement is over the means, or the approach.

Whatever the nature of the conflict between people or

groups, it is valuable to figure out why and how the disagreement developed. Basically, the first step in gaining the cooperation of the other side is to recognize where both of you are positioned on the issues. Just where do you agree and where do you differ? Next, try to analyze how the variance of viewpoint came about. If these differences can be plotted, and *their cause diagnosed,* it is easier to bring the parties together in a collaborative Win-Win negotiation.

In general, the reason we are at odds on an issue may stem from three areas of difference:

1. Experience
2. Information
3. Role

1. Experience

You and I do not see things as they are. We see things as *we* are. Clearly, each person is the product of his or her experience, and no two people can have identical imprinting. Two children of the same sex, one year apart, raised by the same parents, see the world through different lenses. If that's true of these two youngsters raised under the same roof, what about people from totally different environments? To quote journalist Walter Lippmann, "We are all captives of the pictures in our head—our belief that the world we have experienced is the world that really exists."

Therefore, to understand how you think and interpret events I must *get into your world.* To fathom your behavior, I must try to elicit your feelings, attitudes, and belief system.

In the vernacular of today's young, I've got to know "where you're coming from."

2. Information

Ordinarily, people have been exposed to different data and have acquired different facts along the way. There are always things "on my sheet of paper," to use a figure of speech, that are not contained on yours, and vice versa. From this information in our possession, each of us will make deductions and conclusions, frame issues, and determine a course of action.

Obviously, if we are working from a different information base, we will end up poles apart. If an approaching conflict is to be minimized, we must be willing to share this knowledge with each other. This would include not just financial details, but relevant ideas, feelings, and needs as well. The only way you can expect someone to understand your point of view is to provide them with the substance from which your outlook was developed. Essentially then, the task is education and not argumentation!

3. Role

Very often divergent views are a result of the part you have been given to play in the negotiation drama. The role or job you have affects how you perceive the situation and colors your view of what might constitute an equitable settlement. All things being equal, a prosecutor and a defense attorney can honestly advocate very different positions.

No matter whom you represent, there is a tendency for you to be morally directed—to believe, "The angels are on my side, for I represent the forces of good, against the forces of evil." Such a pose is, of course, ridiculous. It's also self-defeating. If a negotiation is to be successful some of this emotional content must be drained. Both sides must learn to say, "If I were in their place, representing that constituency, maybe I would take a similar position."

Believe me, this attitude will not cause you to defect to the opposition. Somehow, no matter how empathetic you act, you will never forget who signs your paycheck. But thinking this way will help you to recognize the other party's constraints, problems, and real needs. Having this outlook is the key to creative problem solving.

Before going any further, let's summarize the negotiation approach being outlined in this chapter.

The emphasis is *not* upon slick maneuvers that finesse or manipulate the other side; rather, it's on the development of genuine relationships based upon trust, where both sides win.

We have been saying that all people are unique but not that complex—they merely wish to satisfy their needs. If my needs are different from yours, we are not really adversaries. Therefore, if I can use the right method and manner in approaching you, and we can transform the shape of things to meet mutual needs, both of us can emerge victorious.

Successful collaborative negotiation lies in finding out what the other side really wants and showing them a way to get it, while you get what you want.

It's not over until it's over.
                    —Yogi Berra

9. More on the Win-Win technique

Accomplishing mutual satisfaction using the collaborative Win-Win style involves emphasis on three important activities:

1. Building trust
2. Gaining commitment
3. Managing opposition

1. Building trust

By now you must realize that I do *not* share the cynical view that people are inescapably greedy or evil. Without underestimating the difficulty of developing trust in a competitive society, experience has shown me that it can be done. In a *continuing relationship*, the more trust you place in others, the more they will justify your faith. Convey your belief in their honesty and reliability and you will encourage them to live up to these expectations.

What is the alternative? Start out suspicious and distrustful and surely you will have your prophecy fulfilled. Thus, the only way to save ourselves from the worst may just be to expect the best.

And the best is a *trusting relationship,* in which each party has a firm belief in the honesty and reliability of the other. It's a mutual dependence—a potential alliance to deal with inevitable disagreement. It's a climate that lays the foundation for transforming conflict into satisfying outcomes.

This mutual trust is the mainspring of collaborative Win-Win negotiations. Let's discuss now how and when this relationship can be established. For reasons that will become evident, I have divided the activity of building trust into two time frames:

A. The process stage
B. The formal event

A. *The process stage*

Previously, in distinguishing between the process stage and the formal event, we used the analogy of mental illness. As you will recall, we said that this condition develops—or is in process—over an extended period. This measure of time would always precede the formal event, in which the patient is diagnosed and certified as mentally ill. The point made was that a negotiation is also a continuous process concluding with a formal interaction between the parties. Therefore, when we say, "The negotiation will begin on March 5 at 2:00 P.M.," we are referring only to the formal event.

This final step in the negotiation process usually takes the form of a personal meeting between the parties, but it could also occur by telephone or even by way of written messages. Most people persist in thinking that this last stage of the process *is the negotiation.* However, every concluding formal event is preceded by weeks or months of lead time contained in the process stage of a negotiation.

This concept, which recognizes that the formal event is

merely the culmination of a lengthy process, has broad application to everyday life. Whether producing a delicious homemade cake or taking a final examination, the success of these events depends upon forethought and timely enterprise.

To illustrate further, here's another analogy:

Your daughter and future son-in-law wish to have a formal church wedding and a large reception afterward. As the happy parents of the bride, you agree to make the arrangements and foot the bill. Although the formal event will encompass only a seven-hour period, the preparation will consume a process stage of six months.

Fortunate people are by definition those whom fortune favors—but they are favored because they effectively use their lead time during the process stage. In baking a cake, taking a final exam, or planning a wedding, the efforts expended early determined the final result.

By the same token, it is choice, not chance, that determines the ultimate outcome of a negotiation. Circumstances do not evolve by chance—they are brought about by action or, more often, by inaction during the process stage. It is then, *prior to* the actual bargaining event, that attitudes are shaped, confidence established, and expectations developed. Should the negotiation event produce a harvest of discord, the likelihood is that the seeds were sown and cultivated during the process stage. As Benjamin Disraeli said, "We make our fortunes and call them fate."

Therefore, fortune will favor the person who uses his lead time to seed an environment of trust that will grow and ripen during the event. This ability, to use the present in anticipation of the future, will make the difference.

Before the conflict has been formalized is when you can impact most effectively on the other side's attitude. As I indicated, once the red light glows on the TV camera, the other side is often on guard and becomes reluctant to expose anything that will increase their vulnerability.

Before the process has become a formal event your actions

and behavior are taken at face value. But once an event has crystallized, anything you do is often viewed as a ploy, a gambit or a gimmick, especially in a competitive environment.

Let me exaggerate to elaborate upon this point.

You and I meet for the first time during the event, in what could be a prolonged competitive negotiation. Supposing you offer me a cup of coffee and a cigarette, even though you yourself abstain. What will my reaction be? If there's no trust in our relationship, I might be thinking, "What's his motive? Is he trying to soften me up?" Conceivably, if I were even more suspicious I might think, "This guy is trying to keep me awake at night. Maybe he wants me to get emphysema!" Obviously, if you made the same offer prior to the event, I would regard it as a gracious gesture from a considerate person.

In short, there are certain actions prior to the event that will give you pluses, goodwill, and credit. Yet during the event in an adversary climate, those same actions will result in minuses, cocked eyebrows, and debits.

Therefore, you must make effective use of the process stage of a negotiation. You cannot afford to wait until the actual confrontation or event. Use this lead time to analyze and diagnose the cause of the potential disagreement. Earlier we said that conflict may arise from differences in *experience, information,* or the *role* we have.

Take action *before* the formal event in these three areas to narrow the variance of viewpoint and to build trust. Constantly hold in your mind a picture of the trusting, problem-solving climate that you would like to see when the event ultimately takes place and take action to bring it about.

Our world may be one of walking paranoia, but *trust is the universal lubricant.* No one will ever tell you anything worthwhile unless you are trusted with that information. No one will ever make an agreement with you that they intend to keep unless they trust you. So use the process stage to build relationships based upon trust.

B. *The formal event*

Once a relationship of trust has been established, it elicits recognition of mutual vulnerability, it prevents disruptive conflict from developing, and it encourages the sharing of information. The evolution to this climate will change attitudes, affect expectations, and transform gladiators into problem solvers. If the process stage was used to bring about this transformation, the parties will approach the formal event seeking a solution that will satisfy everyone's needs.

At the outset of the formal event, continue to build upon the common ground and establish trust. Start off with a positive approach that will get immediate agreement on all sides. If the event is a group meeting, you might say, "Ladies and gentlemen, can we agree on why we are here? How does this strike you? . . . To fashion a fair and equitable solution to this situation that all of us can live with?"

Obviously, you are not asking for feedback, but your framing of the problem or goal is bound to generate assent. Why, your statement is the equivalent of asking for approval of apple pie, the flag, and a hot lunch for orphans!

The initial focus of the discussion should always be on getting agreement to this general statement of the problem. If you can get everyone looking to this end result, they will spend their energy and creativity searching for different alternatives and new ways that might accommodate the needs of all concerned.

Conversely, if you start out talking about means or alternatives, as in "my way versus your way," you will quickly get bogged down in disagreement. From this point, demands and counter-demands follow, and the next step is that the group is polarized into winners and losers.

Thus, by keeping the emphasis on ends and not means, those involved will move from general disagreement to general agreement. This will reduce anxiety, defuse hostility, and encourage freer communication of facts, feelings, and needs.

In such a creative climate a broad range of new alternatives will develop, enabling everyone to get what they want.

Let me give you an example of this. About a year ago, when conducting a bit of business in Ames, Iowa, I had dinner at a restaurant with a couple I've known for a long time. I'll call them Gary and Janet. After we examined the menu I asked, "What's wrong? If you don't mind my saying so, you both seem a little tense."

Gary fiddled with his fork. "You won't believe this, Herb, but we're having trouble deciding where to go on our two-week vacation this year. I want to go to northern Minnesota, or possibly Canada. Janet wants to go to play tennis at a resort in Woodlands, Texas—"

"Our high school son, who's so crazy about water he's like the Creature from the Black Lagoon, wants to go to the Lake of the Ozarks in southern Missouri," interjected Janet. She added, "Our grade school son wants to see the Adirondacks again, because he has a thing about mountains . . . and our daughter, who's a junior in college, doesn't care if she goes anywhere this year."

"How come?" I asked.

"Because she yearns for peace and quiet," grumbled Gary. "She'd like to bask in the sun in our backyard and study for her Law School Aptitude Test. But we don't want to leave her home alone."

"Hmmm . . ." I said. "You're sure all over the lot geographically. Minnesota, Texas, the Adirondacks, the Lake of the Ozarks, and your backyard are about as far apart as you can get."

"You'd think it would be fun, discussing a vacation, but all we do is *argue!* Talk about conflict! Gary here doesn't want to go to Texas because he can't stand air conditioning."

"Can you blame me?" said Gary. "I have an air conditioner breathing down my neck five months out of the year! It makes my muscles ache. I also can't stand humidity, and Texas is humid."

"That's not all," continued Janet. "My beloved husband doesn't want to wear a jacket and tie to dinner—and I, for one, plan to dine out at a nice restaurant every evening. I'm tired of being the chief cook and bottle washer!"

"I plan to be casual this year," said Gary. "I want to play golf while you play tennis and then not have to change again for a meal. By the way, our high school son doesn't want to dress for dinner either. All he wants to do is walk around in his jeans."

"Are you going to drive or take a plane?" I asked, mentally fitting their information tidbits together.

"We're going to drive," said Gary. "I'm a white-knuckle flyer."

"But once we get to where we're going," Janet said, "I don't intend to get in the car until we're ready to come back. I spend too much of my time, whatever the season, acting as an unpaid chauffeur."

After our waiter queried us, then jotted down our entrées, I said, "if you'll pardon my saying this—and I think I *can* say it, because I've known you for a long time—I have a feeling you may be approaching this problem the wrong way."

"I'm all ears," said Gary, fiddling with his fork.

"What you ought to try," I said, "is to find a solution all of you can not only live with, but be happy with."

"How?" asked Janet, grinding out her cigarette.

"From what I hear," I said, "all five of you are acting like adversaries, rather than collaborative problem solvers." I turned to Gary. "According to your comments, your needs are to play golf, not dress for dinner, and get away from both air conditioning and humidity."

"Right," he said.

I turned to Janet. "According to your comments, your needs are to play tennis, eat out, and not have to drive a car."

"True," she assented.

"Your real needs aren't necessarily to go to Texas or

Canada. Those are means or alternatives that you think will satisfy your needs."

They both pursed their lips.

Gesturing to a bus boy to bring us more water, I continued, "Your youngest child wants to see mountains; your middle child wants to swim, fish, or do both; and your oldest child wants to study for an aptitude test. Are all those individual needs incompatible?"

"I don't know," said Gary. "Maybe not."

"Listen, I know your family, and you all like and trust each other. So you are already halfway home. Have you tried having a collaborative Win-Win session with the whole family, where you first get agreement on the general problem?"

"Not really," admitted Janet.

"Why don't you try it after you leave here?" I suggested. "Huddle with each other and your kids and ask for their help in solving the family's problem. Don't discuss individual alternatives or means at the beginning, but keep the focus on the end result. In other words, 'How can we satisfy everyone?' "

Gary cocked an eyebrow. "What do you say, Janet? Want to give it a try? You're much more tactful than I am. You should be chairman of the family discussion."

Janet shrugged. "All right. I'm game."

A month and a half later, Gary phoned me at my office and blurted, "Herb! It worked!"

"What worked?" I asked.

"The collaborative solution to our vacation!"

"Good," I grunted. "Where did you go?"

"To the Manor Vail Lodge in Colorado," Gary said. "We did exactly as you suggested. Everyone got together, and we all shared our feelings and desires. Then we got travel folders and looked for a solution that would satisfy all our needs. From this discussion we came up with Vail, Colorado."

"Why Vail?" I asked.

"Because it met *all* our needs. You were right about Texas, Canada, and all that. They're great places, apparently, but this place seemed to really fill the bill for all of us. On paper, that is. And when we got there, it *did*. Tennis courts for Janet, golf course for me, really big mountains for the little guy, plenty of swimming and fishing for my high school kid (he even went white-water rafting), no air conditioning, because there's no humidity during the day and it's cool at night, ample peace and quiet for my studious daughter, no need to drive our car, because there were shuttle buses—and, though we dined out every night, I didn't have to dress for dinner! How about that?"

"Great," I said. "You also apparently enjoyed your pre-vacation brainstorming session!"

"You bet," said Gary. "It brought all of us closer together. When are you coming to Ames again?"

"The very next time I get the itch for action," I said, grinning.

"You're okay, Herb—you certainly know the mechanics of fixing things," he said.

"Not really, Gary. As you know, I'm mechanically inept. Even when I try hard to put my foot in my mouth I sometimes miss. However, the way *you* solved *your* problem was okay."

That phone call made my day, because I like to see people who are in continuing relationships collaborate to resolve conflict creatively.

In the Gary, Janet, and family situation, everyone emerged victorious. The "Where shall we go?" negotiation wasn't approached as an adversary encounter. Concern was exhibited for each person's feelings and needs. Individual needs were harmonized and reconciled. All acted in a collaborative mode, rather than a competitive mode. The five gladiators were transformed into problem solvers. Because the brainstorming session emphasized ends, not means, a fair and equitable solution was arrived at—a solution that delighted everyone.

I wasn't at the brainstorming session, but I'll bet my bottom dollar that the formal event was kicked off with a positive approach that got immediate agreement on all sides.

Ordinarily, where continuing relationships exist, there's adequate lead time available before a negotiating event—lead time in which you can build trust.

However, life being what it is, there *are* instances in which you cannot or do not anticipate a negotiating event that suddenly looms before you. Instead of anticipating the event and and preparing for it, the way you'd like to, you're dumped into it, head over heels. In such a circumstance, can you establish the confidence and faith required to produce a Win-Win outcome? The answer is yes, if you size up the situation correctly. Even without a process stage, you can use the event itself to probe for information and establish a relationship that will yield a favorable outcome for both sides. Let me share with you what happened to me not too long ago.

After some discussion during my absence, my family decided that our lifestyle was inadequate unless graced with the presence of a videotape recorder—to be exact, an RCA VHS Selecta-Vision, plus a twenty-one-inch Sony TV set with a remote control. When I arrived home late one Friday night, I was summarily informed that I'd been selected, based upon qualifications, to buy these items the following morning. Mine is a democratic family, so no matter how I protested, the scales were tipped four to one against me.

Actually, I was protesting not the request itself, but only the timing. I planned to use a videotape recorder in a new business venture and had been thinking for some time of gauging its effectiveness. Nevertheless, after spending an entire week in an exasperating negotiation overseas, I didn't relish the thought of facing off with a department store clerk or a local shop owner.

But I did. After all, one must maintain one's status in one's family. The biggest problem I had was time. All the local stores open at 9:00 A.M. Since I was taking my youngest to a college football game at 11:00 A.M., I didn't have much of an interval in which to gather information, use time effectively, and exercise power.

Fortunately, I knew my needs. They were to acquire the product at a reasonable price and to have it delivered and installed in good working order. The latter need is especially important for me, since I am the person who once spent 3½ hours putting together a three-piece bird feeder.

While driving into town, I said to myself, "Herb, you don't want to get a great deal; just don't end up in the *Guinness Book of Records* for buying the most expensive standard videotape recorder. So play it cool."

Acting as though I had all the time in the world—so cool as to be virtually catatonic—I casually entered the establishment at 9:20 A.M. "Hi," I said to the proprietor.

"Hello there," he replied. "Can I help you?"

"Well, I don't know," I responded. "I'm just looking around."

Since I was the only customer in the store and seemed to have a lot of time I started up a friendly conversation. I asked, in an offhand manner, how the new shopping center in the neighborhood was affecting his business.

"Well," he vouched, "there's been a slump due to it, because it just opened. But I think business will come back—you know how things are. People want to see what the center's all about, you know? But they'll soon get tired of it, don't you think?"

I nodded in agreement.

He continued, "Eventually, I believe, old customers will return."

While looking at clock radios and TV sets, and expressing some interest in videotape recorders, I continued to ask questions and build a relationship. I told him where I lived and how important I thought the local merchants were to the community.

Wiping his mouth with the back of one hand, he murmured, "I wish more residents of this town felt that way."

As I listened with empathy, he started to talk about his problems. "I don't know why people in this town always have to use those plastic charge cards. You'd think the government doesn't print enough money. It costs *me* whenever *they* charge."

While continuing our amicable discourse I ran my fingers over a videotape recorder. "Hmm . . ." I interjected. "How does this thing work? I'm all thumbs, you know. I don't even know the difference between AC and DC."

He showed me how it worked. "Here's an example," he said. "Before that shopping center opened, some executives would buy two or three of these at one time for their business. But lately nothing!"

Following this I asked, "Oh, if they buy more than one, you give a discount like the big stores?"

"Oh yes," he said, his eyes visibly sparkling. "I do sell items cheaper in quantity."

After showing specific interest in the videotape recorders and receiving a fifteen-minute demonstration, I inquired, "Which would you personally recommend?"

Without hesitation he stated, "Why, this RCA is your best bet. I have one myself."

It was now almost 9:45 A.M., and we were on a first-name basis, Herb and John. We had a relationship going, and I knew a great deal about his needs and problems.

Now, with the foundation in place, I said, with the humility of Oliver Twist hesitantly asking for a bowl of gruel, "Look . . . I don't know what these things cost. In fact, I haven't the *faintest* idea. But John, I want to encourage you to stay in business. You know your costs. Tell you what I'm going to do, John—I'm going to rely on you. Just as I trust your recommendation as to the best model, so I'll trust you when it comes to a fair price. I'm *not* going to quibble with you in any way. Whatever number you come up with—whatever you write down as a fair price—I'll pay you right now!"

"Thank you, Herb," John said, genuinely pleased.

I continued, still casual, still fairly offhand, "I rely on your honesty, John. I feel I know you. I won't question any figure you come up with, even though I realize I can probably better it by shopping around at various department stores."

John wrote down a figure, though he shielded it from me with his right hand.

"I want you to make a reasonable profit, John . . . but, of course, I want to get a reasonable deal myself."

At this point, I introduced more information. (Remember, I'd entered his shop with instructions to also purchase a twenty-one-inch Sony color TV set, complete with remote control.) I said, "Wait a second . . . *what if* I also got this Sony with remote control? Would that have a bearing on the total price?"

"You mean as a package deal?"

"Yes, I thought about it based upon what *you* said earlier," I said softly.

"Of course," he murmured. "Just one second while I add up all these numbers."

When he was finally ready to give me the total price, I said, "There's just one more thing I should mention to you. I expect that what I am paying you is fair—a transaction where we both profit. Should that be the case, when my business makes a smiliar purchase in three months, you have *already made* that sale."

As I continued to talk, I noticed that he crossed out the price he had written. "But John, if I should find out that my trust was misplaced, this disappointment will prevent me from giving you any additional business."

"Of course," he murmured. "Let me go into the back room for a minute. I'll be right back."

After consulting a book, he returned in a minute and a half and scrawled another figure.

Following on what he had said earlier, I now ventured, "I was thinking about what you said a few minutes ago. You know—about your cash-flow problem. That gave me an idea I hadn't thought of before. I was going to charge all this, but . . . would it be more convenient for you if I paid you in *cash?*"

"Oh, yes," he replied. "That would help a great deal. Especially now." Saying this, he jotted another number on his pad.

I tugged my lower lip. "You'll install this for me, right? I won't be in town, you know."

"Oh, yes," he said. "I'll install it for you."

"Okay," I said. "Give me your price."

He gave me the package price for the RCA and the Sony. It totaled $1,528.30—which I later learned represented an equitable collaborative transaction.

I strode to a bank three doors away, made out a check for that amount, cashed it, and returned to John with the money in my hand. It was now 10:05 A.M—mission accomplished!

All right: What happened here? How did I come out the way I did, though I was unprepared? How did I escape being victimized, in what might have been a competitive situation?

The Specific "Game Plan":

1. *Establish trust.* Because my initial approach was sincere, casual, friendly, and relaxed I set the tone for the seller to respond in kind.
2. *Obtain information.* I asked questions, listened with empathy, and conveyed understanding.
3. *Meet his needs.* Both my approach—the process—and the way I packaged my offers were directed at meeting the store owner's unique needs.
4. *Use his ideas.* I was often "piggybacking" on the ideas that the seller had mentioned earlier.

5. *Transform relationship to collaboration*. My main emphasis was to have the merchant see me as a continuing customer and not as a one-time buyer.

6. *Take moderate risk*. Although I was prepared to accept the price as given, my risk was minimal. By building a relationship, giving information slowly, and using the power of morality and the option of the future, I considerably reduced the risk.

7. *Get his help*. By getting the seller's involvement, I used his data and knowledge of costs to solve *our* problem.

John not only installed the equipment beautifully, but he also gave me a free stand for the videotape recorder—a stand I hadn't thought of asking for. Oh yes, two months later I fulfilled my commitment, when a second purchase was made for my business. Since this episode, we have become friends and have a close, trusting relationship.

In substance, once trust exists it tends to endure. You may have observed that many people fall out of love; yet rarely does anyone fall out of like. Where trust is lacking you are attempting to build the foundation of an agreement on quicksand. To cite an example, you may see political contenders try to come together in the euphoric last stage of a national political convention. Without an underpinning of trust, the framework of these negotiations collapses. Therefore, if you want a successful outcome that results in mutual commitment, the first order of business is building trust. The sooner the better!

2. Gaining commitment

No individual is an isolated entity. Everyone that you deal with is being reinforced by those around them. From your banker to your boss, they are receiving encouragement to maintain their current position. Even the so-called leaders, whether a head of state or the head of a household, have an organization behind them shaping their decisions. In fact, leadership is often the ratification of decisions that were already made.

Assume that you need your boss's permission to get something you want. In trying to persuade him, you have come to the conclusion that he is stubborn beyond belief. You mutter to yourself, "This guy is unbelievable, inhuman. Talking to him is like talking into a dead phone. Maybe there's something wrong with his genes!"

The solution to this problem may not be docile submission to authority, getting him to take a genetic examination, or even a continuance of the frontal attack. The answer may lie in finding out who's important to the boss and getting those people to help you influence him. Gaining the commitment of these people to your idea will do wonders—even with the most obstinate boss.

Excepting hermits and recluses, everyone has an organization. It's true of your boss, and it's true of you. If I see you in context, you are connected to a web of relationships. These are the people that you listen to and talk to—on the .job and at home. You have friends, subordinates, associates, peers, and acquaintances whose opinions you value and respect—those you care about; individuals who carry weight because you might need them in the future. This network comprises your organization. You may be the hub or core, but the bodies rotating about you influence your behavior.

If I can somehow sway your organization, their movement may divert you from your original course. Think about it for a moment. Why do you do certain things? Why do you live where you live? Why do you drive a particular model car? Were these decisions yours alone, or did your organization, whatever its constituency, influence your behavior? If you're leveling with yourself, you'll concede that many of your choices were already made—at least in part—by others. You may often lead, as I often lead, by following in front.

Emerson once said, "Things are in the saddle and they ride mankind." Let me give you an episode from my own experience, where I exercised leadership very much like a wooden figurehead on a Norse ship:

Several years ago I lived in a rustic community in northern Illinois called Libertyville. I had five acres of rolling land, tall oak trees, and a nine-room custom-built home. I thought I was really happy there—until my wife explained to me one morning that we weren't that happy. She said, "The value system here isn't right for us. There's no public transportation. What's more, the children aren't being properly educated in the local schools." I rubbed my chin and finished my coffee, and we decided to move.

Since I was away from home a great deal, the house-hunting responsibility fell on my wife's shoulders. They slumped when she realized, first hand, how the real estate market had changed in seven years. It's one thing to read about skyrocketing prices; it's something else to confront them personally.

Though despondent, my wife continued the futile search for two months. Throughout her ordeal I remained cheerful—since *I* was not looking. During the weekends, to raise her spirits, I said such things as, "Keep up the good work! All of your efforts will eventually pay off," and "A stitch in time saves nine!"

Somehow these aphorisms didn't help our relationship. As a reaction to my attitude, she decided that I required sensitivity training. To sensitize me to the realities of the market-place, she involved me, weekends, in looking at rejected homes.

I'd come home late each Friday night and collapse in bed, hoping to get some needed sleep. It wasn't in the cards. My wife awakened me at dawn, gave me a cup of coffee, then trotted me around all day Saturday examining homes. She repeated the process on Sunday, until it was time for me to leave for the airport. I suffered through this schedule three weekends in a row.

Finally, footsore and exasperated, I blurted, "Look—you claim you want self-actualization, self-fulfillment, and more responsibility. You're a liberated woman! Why don't *you* buy the house? And when you buy it, you let me know. You send me a memo, and I'll be happy to move in with you and the children!" I paused, reflected, then continued, "In fact, I don't even know why *I'm* looking at all, because I don't even live at home that much." In other words, I "put the ball in her court"!

During the next couple of weeks I knew she was looking. It didn't bother me that she was—because I wasn't. That is, until that fateful week.

When I'm on the road, which is most of the time, I call home every night. Admittedly, I'm not a creative telephone conversationalist. Over the years, I have fallen into a rut in my phone discussions. My standard opener is always the same, "Hi—how's everything?" And my preferred answer is always "Fine!" I then follow that with, "What's new?" and my preferred answer is always "Nothing!"

Now we come to the portentous week. My broken-record dialogue was repeated on Monday, Tuesday, and Wednesday evenings—all with the standard questions and the preferred responses. On Thursday evening, I phoned and once again asked, "Hi—how's everything?"

My wife replied, "Fine."

"What's new?" I continued. (What could be new? I just talked to her last night.)

She replied, "I bought a house."

"*What?* Say that again."

"Oh, I bought a house," she said casually.

"Look," I interjected, "I believe you are semantically incorrect. What you meant to say was that you *saw* a house that you liked."

"Right," she said. "And I bought it."

A lump was forming in my throat. "No, no, you mean that you saw a house that you liked and you made an offer on the house that you liked."

"Right," she said. "And they accepted it, and we got it."

I swallowed hard. "You b-b-b-bought a house? A *whole* house? You couldn't have!"

"Oh yes," she stated matter-of-factly. "It was really easy. . . . You'll love it. It's an English Tudor style. Sixteen rooms. Fifty-five years old. It overlooks Lake Michigan."

A pain shot through my shoulder and down my left arm. I stammered, over and over, "You b-b-b-bought a house."

"Yes!" emphasized my partner.

Finally, realizing I was under stress, she lowered her voice and added, "I *did* write on the contract that the purchase is subject to your approval."

The pain in my left arm subsided somewhat. "You mean, if I don't approve, you can get out of it?"

"Of course," my wife assured me. "We have till ten o'clock Saturday morning. If you really dislike the set-up, we can get out of it. It just means I have to start looking all over again."

I arrived home late Friday night and got up nice and early. The wife and I were going to see this home that *she thought* she might have bought. However, it was I, the alleged technical titular leader of the household, who was personally going to the scene to make the command decision. We both moved out smartly into the "command car," technical titular leader at the wheel, my associate beside me.

We drove along, and I said to my wife, "By the way, does anybody know about this house you *almost* bought?"

"Oh yes," she said.

"Who could possibly know? It just happened!"

"Many people," she responded.

"Who?" I persisted.

"Well, all our neighbors and friends know, for starters. In fact, they are throwing us a gala farewell party tonight."

My jaw muscles tightened. "What do you mean for starters? Who else could know?"

"Well, our families know—your family and my family. In fact, my mother has already ordered custom-made drapes for the living room. I called in the measurements to her."

While my stomach knotted I wheeled around a corner.

"Who else knows?"

"Well, the children know. They told their friends, they told their teachers; they selected the bedrooms they want. Sharon and Steven have even ordered furniture for their new rooms from a department store."

"What about our dog?" I asked, trying to prevent a vein on my forehead from throbbing.

"Oh, Fluffy's been there, sniffing around as only Fluffy can. She likes the neighborhood's fire hydrants, and a cute male dog down the block caught her eye."

What was happening here? The organization was moving away from the leader, that's what! It was the Zig Zag Theory of Organizational Behavior. As you know, all organizations start down the road, shoulder-to-shoulder. Everyone's in lock step—everyone's together. When suddenly, without warning, the troops all abruptly zig and then zag.

When that happens, the leader is left stranded in left field, muttering, "What happened? Where'd they all go? Where is everyone?" This phenomenon is known as loneliness—without a cigarette.

In my case, the alleged technical titular leader was now lonely in the zig, with his organization having zagged away. What do you think the alleged technical titular—now lonely —leader did under these circumstances? You're so right. He ratified a decision that was already made, to keep the title of alleged technical titular leader.

It often seems that my wife knows more about negotiations than I do. She understands that *when the body moves, the head is inclined to follow*.

What my spouse did was obtain commitment to her decision

from the people who are important to me. She put into practice the old saying that "it is often easier to ask forgiveness than permission." She presented me with a *fait accompli*, an accomplished fact. To sustain the appearance—even the self-concept—of leadership, I followed in front. In putting my signature on the agreement, I merely ratified a decision that was already made by my wife, our children, our families, our friends and neighbors, and of course our dog, Fluffy.

Never see anyone as an isolated unit. See those whom you wish to persuade in context, as a central core around which others move. Get the support of those others and you will influence the position and movement of the core.

3 Dealing with opposition

To progress to your place in the sun you must always put up with some blisters—those who dispute your right of passage. There is nothing wrong with having this opposition. From it, you sharpen your mind, increase your skill, and add zest to your life. In fair competition with an opponent you gain insight into yourself that will foster growth and development. As Walt Whitman wrote, "Have you not learned great lessons from those who braced themselves against you?"

Opposition is what life is all about. Your entire muscular system depends on it. When an infant first tries to stand he encounters resistance from the force of gravity and falls down. But as he persists, he builds the muscles in his arms, legs, and back until he finally rises. Dealing with opposition can keep you alert.

To get what you want, you have to encounter opposition. If you have no opponents, it may be that you're still seated. In essence, you're not negotiating to get the result you want. Provided that you are doing nothing, you'll soon get opponents. Your boss, peers, subordinates, mate, family, and others will oppose you because of your inaction. You may even end up negotiating with yourself, as you try to manage your disappointment. So the question isn't whether you will have opposition. The question is, "From whence cometh your opposition?"

Opposition comes in two forms:

> A. Idea opponents
> B. Visceral opponents

A. *Idea opponents*

An idea opponent is one who disagrees with you on a particular issue or alternative. The disparity of misunderstanding is theoretical. You say, "I think it should be done *this* way."

He or she says, "No, I think it should be done *that* way." Approaching this conflict of views, using the method suggested in the previous chapter, it is possible to arrive at a solution that will satisfy both of you.

Remember, our method encourages the pooling of ideas, information, experience, and feelings to find a mutually beneficial outcome. It is even possible, with both sides working together, to bring about a synergistic result. This happens when the final result surpasses the contributions of both sides. Where synergy occurs, "The whole is greater than the sum of its parts," or one plus one equals three. In other words, the final agreement could give both sides more than they even expected at the outset.

When this occurs, you have used the pressure of adversity or opposition to help you get what you want. In this way, an idea opponent is always a potential ally. Granted that a composite solution could be better for you and your opponent, why is this outcome so rarely achieved?

Because most people violate what we have said about building trust and starting with agreement on the problem to be solved. Instead, they begin negotiating with an idea opponent by announcing *their* alternative or answer. They may even take a harder line and express *their* conclusion as a demand or ultimatum. Being confronted by your opponent's position, usually stated numerically, causes you to respond in kind. Suddenly, both sides are poles apart in a competitive Win-Lose negotiating mode. The potential ally has suddenly become an adversary.

Should both sides realize their dilemma, they can scrap this framework with its focus on "my way versus your way." Presumably, if too much damage has not been done, they can then share information, redesign the package, and still arrive at a Win-Win conclusion.

But if the focus is not changed, attempts to reconcile the divisive positions are frustrating. Trying to negotiate conclusions or ultimatums is like trying to cut down a redwood tree with a pocket knife. You can jab away forever, but it just stands there. There are no soft spots. There's no give.

Here's what I mean: You apply to me for a job and ask for a salary of $50,000. That's what *you* have concluded you are worth. Based upon my company's pay-grade structure and what others are earning, I offer you $30,000. That's *my* conclusion. You reiterate that $50,000 is your "rock bottom." I restate that $30,000 is my "absolute top." I refuse to budge. You refuse to budge. You won't consider going lower and I won't consider going higher.

To break this impasse and in a spirit of harmony, I say, "Okay, maybe I can go to $30,200."

Sarcastically, you respond, "Okay, *maybe* I can drop to $49,990."

We butt our heads together with the force of two mountain goats on a cliff.

"Is that it?" you finally ask.

"That's it," I reply.

You depart in a huff and start looking elsewhere. Somewhat irritated, I open my top desk drawer and begin to leaf through a pile of résumés.

But what if—as idea opponents—we started out searching for a solution to the problem of meeting both of our needs? Gradually, as we build trust we share information, experience, feelings and needs with each other. As we progress each of us has heard the other's point of view and is able to see things from his angle as well as our own. We now can understand their constraints, and when each party eventually states his salary position, we can comprehend the rationale behind it.

In spite of all this effort expended, a logjam continues to exist, and we are far apart on salary. Supposing I now pour both of us a glass of water from a container and suggest, "Maybe, we can move off the discussion of salary itself and talk about other forms of compensation that might meet your particular needs."

You nod your head in assent. Together, we proceed to repackage or rework the agreement, taking into account my restrictions, limitations, and needs as well as yours. What we are doing is moving from the competitive Win-Lose area of salary where I am confined, to use leverage in other areas where I have more flexibility.

After a candid give-and-take discussion, we set up a situation in which although you receive only $30,000 in salary, you get money in other forms. The final accord calls for you to receive more than the equivalent of $20,000 in terms of:

1. A company car
2. An expense account
3. A country-club membership
4. Profit sharing
5. A free vested contribution to your retirement fund
6. A low-interest loan
7. A free medical plan
8. A subsidized dental plan
9. Free life insurance
10. A hospitalization plan that's 85 percent company funded

11. Future educational opportunities for yourself
12. Stock options
13. Additional time off
14. An extra week of vacation
15. Control over your own budget
16. A new office with a window
17. Your own designated parking space
18. Educational opportunities for your children
19. Relocation expenses
20. A bonus upon completion of each successful project
21. Your own secretary
22. Two inches of additional foam under your carpeting, so you can spring about
23. The company purchase of your old home, if necessary
24. An all-expenses-paid annual trip to attend the Industry Association's convention in Hawaii
25. A small royalty percentage on the new products developed

Clearly, I have gone beyond the realm of realism in any employment contract that I know about. This listing was deliberately expanded to give you an idea of how dollar bills, or in some cases personal satisfaction, can come in forms other than salary.

It should be noted that such items cost the company money, but it may be in an area where the expenditure is more acceptable from their point of view. Finally, unlike salary, some of these benefits are not legally taxed as income. And so the real worth and value of an item given to you in this manner is much greater than if you were to pay for it yourself. You have just experienced a synergistic effect.

Keep in mind that these twenty-five extras represent an incomplete listing, and some are of greater or lesser value to you, depending on your unique needs. They are nothing more than dollar bills in a different form or dispensed in a different manner.

If you were the prospective job applicant, this refashioned and reshaped package might meet your needs much better than the $50,000 in salary. Assuming that this creative agreement was within reason, don't feel sorry for the employer; an experienced buyer of services generally gets value for his or her expenditure.

That was a hypothetical example of reconstructing a negotiation to meet the needs of idea opponents. Here's a real one:

Several years ago, I represented a large corporation that was attempting to purchase a coal mine in eastern Ohio. The mine owner was a tough negotiator who wanted $26 million from the outset. A $15 million offer was made as a starter.

"Are you kidding?" blustered the owner.

The corporation answered in effect, "No, we're not! But give us your realistic selling price, and we'll consider it."

The mine owner remained adamant at $26 million.

In the ensuing months the buyer offered $18 million, $20 million, $21 million, and $21½ million, but the seller refused to budge. Stalemated, neither side moved. The situation? A $21½ million offer against a $26 million demand. As I stated before, it is almost impossible to creatively negotiate only conclusions. Since you have no information about needs, it is difficult to restructure or reshape the package.

Perplexed as to why the owner wouldn't accept what appeared to be a fair offer, I had dinner with him evening after evening. Each time we ate, I explained how reasonable the company was in making their current offer. The seller was usually taciturn or changed the subject. One night in responding to my regular pitch, he commented, "You know, my brother got $25½ million and some extras for his mine."

"Aha!" I thought. "That's the reason he's locked in on that particular number. He's got other needs that we are apparently neglecting."

With that insight, I huddled with the corporate executives involved and said, "Let's find out exactly what his brother received. Then we can reshape and repackage our proposal. Apparently, we are dealing with important personal needs that have little to do with pure market value."

The corporate officials concurred, and we proceeded along those lines. Shortly thereafter, the negotiation was concluded. The final price fell well within the corporate budget, but the payments and extras were such that the owner felt he had done much better than his brother.

B. *Visceral opponents*

We have observed that *idea opponents* can be addressed on an intellectual level with factual and descriptive comments. In this climate, despite the difference in the initial viewpoint of the parties, creative problem solving can take place.

A *visceral opponent* is an emotional adversary, who not only disagrees with your point of view, but disagrees with you as a human being. He may even attribute sinister or nefarious motives to the position you espouse. In this climate, there is inordinate stress, judgments are formed, accusations may be made, and scorekeeping takes place. Obviously, this is not a fruitful environment in which creative problem solving can take place.

Once you make visceral opponents, they tend to stay with you for a long time, for they are difficult to convert. All the logic, facts, ideas, and evidence you marshal will not be enough. So try not to bring them into being in the first place. Avoid producing a visceral opponent the way you would avoid a contagious disease.

The next obvious question is how you make (or transform) someone into a visceral opponent. Attacking "face" is what causes someone to become an emotional enemy.

Face sense is who I want others to think I am. It's how a person wants to be seen *publicly*. When I am concerned with *my* saving face after a difficult negotiation, I want to make sure that the stature I have always projected in terms of prestige, worth, dignity, and respect will not be diminished.

Self-image, on the other hand, is concerned with how a person sees himself in the *privacy* of his own head. It is who you think you are. The conception that you alone have of yourself, your abilities, your value, and your role.

The two concepts overlap, but only slightly. Briefly, they can be distinguished if we refer to one's *public face sense,* as distinct from one's *private self-image.*

For the sake of further clarification, let's say that in a private discussion I attacked you personally by calling you a fraud, a clown, and a liar. This offensive, though unprovoked attack might have momentarily annoyed you, but your self-image is undoubtedly strong enough to withstand even this abuse.

As you walked away, shaking your head, you might even have thought, "This fellow is not only obnoxious, but he's sick!" In addition, if I came to my senses the next day and sincerely apologized for my aberration, you might even forgive me, since we were the only people involved.

Now let's assume that during a public meeting, or in front of your associates, I made a similar blistering assault, calling you a fraud, a clown, and a liar. Although your self-image would reject my charges as totally unjustified, you will sustain loss of face and wounded pride. At this point you probably will start keeping score, saying to yourself, "That's one, two, or three I owe that creep."

Supposing I were to visit you the next day, begging your forgiveness for my temporary derangement? Chances are that my apology would *not* be accepted. Not only does wounded pride produce a tenacious enemy, but the onslaught was made in public, and I'm trying to make amends in private.

People will go to extreme lengths to avoid loss of face. We all display a remarkable ability to protect ourselves in such situations, from distortion and rationalization to blocking out the episode entirely. In the words of a song that was popular some time ago, "What is too painful to remember, we simply choose to forget."

Ten years ago, I was acquainted with an executive who was unexpectedly fired by his organization after many years of faithful service. He never informed his family or friends of his discharge. Every morning at the usual time, carrying his briefcase, he boarded the train at his suburban station and was transported into Manhattan. Thereafter, he spent endless days in the motion picture houses in Times Square or at the public library, waiting until it was time to catch his regular train home.

It was almost two months before the make-believe world he concocted came apart, when his uninformed wife made an unforeseen phone call to the office. The story is tragic, but it points out the incredible illusions that we are all capable of putting in place to protect our stature in the eyes of the people we care about. In reading the plays of Eugene O'Neill and Tennessee Williams, you will find that this is a recurring theme—the maintenance of make-believe and pipe dreams to protect "face sense."

Keeping in mind the desperate and irrational behavior that individuals may employ to save face, we must avoid any possible public embarrassment to the people with whom we deal. You must train yourself to speak honestly to idea opponents without offending face sense.

You must be able to make your point and present your case without making a visceral enemy. You must always keep in mind the physical law that "for every action there is a reaction." The gist of this was verbalized by Bernard Baruch when he said, "Two things are bad for the heart—running up stairs and running down people."

Emphasizing the consequences and risks involved in making a visceral opponent, two instances come to mind:

The first involves a supervisor named Kate, a competent employee of a large corporation that has an "open-door policy." This doctrine means that if employees believe they have a grievance that is not being rectified by the boss, they have the right of appeal. In effect, they can go over their boss's head and even to the president if necessary. Kate had just cause to believe she was being mistreated by her boss, and after pursuing the matter locally and getting nowhere, she decided to exercise her rights.

She wrote a letter to the president and was flown to the corporate office at the company's expense. There, she met with the division vice-president, who was two levels above her boss in the hierarchy. When the facts of the case were laid out, Kate's immediate boss looked bad.

One week after her return, Kate was summoned to see her boss and his boss. In this session, her boss admitted the error of his ways, promised to rectify her complaint, and asked forgiveness. Thereafter, the matter was resolved to her satisfaction, but the relationship with her superior was never the same.

For starters, he began to point out her mistakes publicly. He kept a written record of her arrival and departure times. In the months that followed, there were minor slights at staff meetings and informational memos that were not received in time for her to make plans and take action. Although she obtained a raise, it was somewhat less than she expected.

Ten months after the "open door" episode, Kate got the message and left "captivity" for a new position that she described to me as "all milk and honey."

The second incident concerns Vince, a social-science teacher and a longtime baseball coach at a metropolitan high school. Because of changing demographics and a minor tax revolt in their district, the principal called a meeting of the entire faculty to discuss where the budget cuts would have to be made. She had an elaborate slide presentation in which her conclusions flowed naturally from the comprehensive data presented. At the conclusion, as she gathered the slides and placed them in her briefcase, she asked the rhetorical question, "Do any of you have any comments?"

At this point, Vince took the unintended bait and pointed out several errors in logic that had been made in selecting the statistics shown. Elaborating further, he made a convincing argument that the principal's conclusions and action plan could not be supported by the evidence she presented.

These statements were particularly telling to this principal, who had an advanced degree in mathematics and who always quoted Michelangelo that "trifles make perfection, but perfection itself is no trifle." Nothing was ever said to him about this brief interlude in his long professional career. However, the next semester Vince was asked to coach soccer instead of baseball, and one year later he was transferred to another high school a greater distance from his home.

As far as I know, Vince is still making the long commute to work. Regarding his career, you might say it's currently stalled. On the road to success, he's parked on the shoulder.

These two cases point out the chances you are taking when you expose someone to ridicule in front of others. Even when you are right, shun all opportunities to humiliate people— at least in public. Remember this, not only for them, but for yourself as well. Ultimately, the avoidance of visceral opposition is the avoidance of *mutual dissatisfaction*.

How can you ensure that you do not make visceral opponents? My two rules are stated in terse negative terms:

1. Never forget the power of your attitude

You will recall that I said earlier that negotiation, whether at work or at home, is a game—"Care, but don't care that much." Even if you have just cause to retaliate, restrain yourself. Remember, the provocative act by itself rarely upsets you; rather, it's the view that you take of it that rankles. No one and nothing can irritate you without your consent. Thomas

Jefferson was alluding to this demeanor when he said, "Nothing gives a person so much advantage over another as to remain always cool and unruffled under all circumstances." Keep saying to yourself over and over, "It's a game. It's the world of illusion. A tactic perceived is no tactic. I care, but not *that* much."

2. Never judge the actions and motives of others

Since you cannot look into someone's heart or mind, it would seem absurd to believe that you might know what impels or propels them. Many times even they don't know.

Furthermore, should you evaluate the information given to you too soon, the speaker may either wind down or clam up.

For example, a child arrives home one evening and casually remarks to his parents, "Hey, Mom, Dad, you know what? I've just been offered a marijuana cigarette!"

"You *what!*" the parents shout in unison, startling their child with the vehemence of their response. Unconsciously, the child lurches backward, and a pregnant pause ensues. Now I ask you, how candid and open will this discussion be?

Forget this particular confrontation, what about the future? Will *this* offspring come back to *these* parents with more information of this type in the months and years ahead? I doubt it.

Why? Because children are sufficiently bright to know that there's no percentage in approaching parents with one problem and leaving with two problems. Should you operate this way in your home or at work, you dry up your sources of information, and your ability to negotiate for the commitment of others becomes greatly impaired.

Perhaps this type of parental outburst is extreme; yet the same kind of negative judgment is often rendered in more familiar ways by the language we use and the cues that accompany it. To illustrate:

Example 1

A parent walks into their child's room and says, "This place looks like a pig sty—oink—oink."

Example 2

A spouse comments to their mate, "You don't give a damn about me! Can't you learn how to scrape the food off your plate before you dump it in the sink?"

Example 3

An exasperated parent shouts to their child, "That zoo music you're blasting on the stereo is so loud, it's polluting the entire neighborhood."

Example 4

A negotiator turns to an opponent across the table and remarks, "Your analysis of these data and the way you are figuring the costs are all wrong."

I should be evident that in all four of these examples the speaker is acting out the role of judge. In each instance, an evaluation is being made of another's lifestyle, values, consideration, integrity, or intelligence.

By no means am I suggesting that you can transform a member of your family into a visceral opponent with a commonplace harangue. What I am saying is that such public utterances can offend and do affect face sense. Moreover, these speech habits are hard to break, and they can carry over to other dealings where trust has not yet been established and the sensitivity is greater.

The elimination of this potential problem is very simple. All that has to be done is the substitution of the word "I" instead of "you" in all these messages. By making use of "I" or "me" you can express your personal feelings, reactions, and needs without sitting in judgment.

Here's how the four examples would read with the incorporation of this simple change:

Example 1
"When this room is not tidy I feel depressed, frustrated, and upset."

Example 2
"I find that when the food is scraped from the plates it takes me half the time to clean up after a meal. This is important to me, since I hate washing dishes."

Example 3
"I am bothered by loud music. I am tired and uptight, and that music is making me irritable."

Example 4
"I must look at data differently than you. I feel that . . ."

We have been saying that some opposition is essential because it results in growth and progress. All progress is derived from opponents—those who are dissatisfied with the *status quo*. It is these people with their different ideas and ways who generate the required tension that leads to creative solutions and new possibilities—the very foundation of progress.

So, cherish your idea opponents as potential allies. Give them your views with sincerity and persistence, without letting your self-esteem ride on the outcome. Though some tension will of course exist, it should be drained of emotional content so that idea opponents are never transformed into visceral opponents.

As you have come to share the concepts and ideas presented in this chapter you can see that I am not talking about a come-on or con game. In a collaborative negotiation, there's no need for conniving, intimidating, fast talking, manipulating, flimflamming, or wheeling and dealing.

On the contrary, I am suggesting a strategy that is oriented toward building and maintaining a continuing relationship. The trusting parties are equals who direct their energies toward solving problems for their mutual benefit. They create a climate of confidence, where the needs of both sides can be fully satisfied and their positions enhanced.

The compromise solution

Unfortunately, many negotiators think that compromise is synonymous with collaboration. It is not. By its very definition, compromise results in an agreement in which each side gives up something it really wanted. It is an outcome where no one fully meets his or her needs.

The strategy of compromise rests on the faulty premise that your needs and mine are always in opposition. And so it is never possible for mutual satisfaction to be achieved. Acting upon this assumption, each of us starts out making an outlandish demand, so that he can ultimately have room to make concessions.

When the pressure builds on both of us to lay aside our differences for the sake of society as a whole, we compromise at a midpoint between our extreme positions. This solution is accepted to avoid a deadlock, but neither of us is really satisfied.

Our needs frustrated, we find some solace in reciting old bromides and clichés: "Half a loaf is better than none," or "Give a little, get a little," or "A good negotiation outcome is one where both sides are somewhat dissatisfied." Needless to say, neither of us feels much obligation to support this arrangement which has not given either side what it really wanted.

If we were to apply "the compromise formula" literally to some of life's negotiation dilemmas the solutions would be ridiculous. Let me show you what I mean with the following simple anecdotes:

Vignette 1

Two graduate students from Seattle, Washington, decide to spend their winter holiday together. He wants to go to Las Vegas, and her preference is Taos, New Mexico. All we know is that each of them has independently arrived at their conclusion.

Let's assume that we can use only the two geographic alternatives in finding a middle-ground solution. If we were to methodically apply the compromise formula the couple would spend their holiday in the vicinity of Polacca on the Hopi Indian reservation in northeast Arizona.

Obviously, I have exaggerated to make my point. By now you realize that if this couple shared information, experience, assumptions, and expectations, a location could be selected that would result in a mutually rewarding trip.

For the sake of argument, if his needs are gambling and big-name entertainment and her needs are downhill skiing and fresh air, options exist (such as Lake Tahoe and Squaw Valley) for both of them to get exactly what they want.

Vignette 2

Recently, I ran across an interesting story dealing with compromise. It was told to me by a friend, who is affectionately known as Big Buddha, "the enlightened one." He goes by this moniker because he once left his wife and infant son to devote himself wholeheartedly to the search for truth. In his case, the noble quest lasted twenty-two hours, but the nickname remained.

Big Buddha recounted a dispute that his two teenage sons had at the conclusion of a Sunday family dinner. The object of their conflict was a leftover baked Idaho potato—not a very big issue in the scheme of things. Each son contended that his claim was superior, and the disagreement intensified.

Playing the role of patriarch, but without getting any information, my friend made the decision for them. In the Buddhist tradition of "middle way," he cut the potato in half and divided it between the sibling rivals. Satisfied with his solution, he adjourned to the living room for serenity of soul —or nirvana via TV.

Later that evening, Big Buddha was advised that his "perfect compromise" had to be renegotiated. It seemed that one son wanted only the skin, whereas his brother desired merely the soft inside of the potato. Obviously, their needs were not in opposition, and the best solution was not a symmetrical compromise.

Vignette 3

As a youngster I shared a bedroom with my older sister. Although the age difference was slight, in intellect and maturity she viewed me from across the great divide. Her serious academic and cultural pursuits contrasted sharply with my activities of closely monitoring the radio adventures of Jack Armstrong and The Shadow.

Because of these dissimilar interests and the limited resource of one bedroom between us, we frequently had conflict over what constituted disturbing and inconsiderate behavior. For months, there were attempts to compromise by "splitting the difference" in our divergent viewpoints or practicing "share and share alike." Even with written schedules and agreements plus parental mediation, the controversy persisted.

Ultimately the matter was resolved when we both came to recognize that considerable time and energy were being wasted as we maneuvered and positioned ourselves for the next mathematical compromise. With recognition of a common interest in solving the problem for our mutual benefit, we were able to think beyond the obvious physical resources of space, hours, and materials. The satisfying solution that met both of our needs was the purchase of earphones for the radio.

Thereafter, I was able to use the radio whenever I chose without disturbing my sister. Chief among the benefits of this solution was that I was listening at the very moment that Kellogg's announced "a once-in-a-lifetime opportunity to send for a Junior G-man Card." In retrospect, this may have been a crucial turning point in my life.

As these examples show, the use of a "statistical compromise formula" will not necessarily result in the successful resolution of conflict. If such an approach is employed "across the board," it causes an increase in game playing, accompanied by now familiar tactical maneuvers, ultimatums, and self-centered adversary behavior.

This is *not* to say that compromise is always a poor choice. Often the strategy of compromise may be appropriate to the particular circumstances. Therefore, you must recognize that once in a while, to be truly effective, you will have to compromise, accommodate, persuade, compete, and even be prepared to walk away.

However, where your relationship with the other side is continuing, you should strive at the outset for a solution that is not just acceptable, but is mutually satisfying. Should circumstances warrant, you may need to alter the course of your initial collaboration to display more accommodation or even competition.

Much like a great chess master, a winning negotiator needs to know every possible strategy from the opening gambit to the end-game play. Then he can enter the event with confidence that he is prepared for every possible eventuality that might occur. Nonetheless, he strives for the best outcome that can give everyone what he wants. And he knows that compromise may be acceptable, but it's not mutually satisfying. It is a back-up, a concluding strategy that he may ultimately have to use to avoid the consequence of a deadlock.

Throughout this chapter, the point has been made that your winning in negotiations does not require someone to lose. Winning means managing the outcome by seeing your reality true and clear and being able to react with the appropriate strategy.

Winning means fulfilling your needs while being consistent with your beliefs and values. Winning means finding out what the other side really wants and showing them a way to get it while you get what you want.

And it is possible for both sides to get what they want, because no two people are identical in terms of likes or dislikes. Each of us is trying to satisfy our needs, but those needs, like our fingerprints, are different.

Ironically as I try to get what I want, only a part of my satisfaction will be derived from acquiring the product, service, right, or thing—the *what* that I am bargaining for. To a much greater extent, my satisfaction will result from the process itself—the *how* of the bargaining encounter. Remember the couple that purchased an antique clock and the way I secured a newspaper in the Miracle on 54th Street? In these episodes, the nature of the process was what fulfilled needs and determined satisfaction.

It is this individuality and the meeting of needs through the process itself that causes us all to do silly things. Have you ever observed people returning from a tropical winter vacation? Away for just two weeks, they stand in a customs line at a northern airport. They are wearing Hawaiian shirts and muumuus, holding huge sombreros, or carrying stuffed alligators. Whenever I see them, I start to smile. But then, I recollect that I myself am the owner of a Mexican *serape!*

Do you know what a *serape* is? It's a shawl, a poncho, a bright-colored woolen blanket that Mexicans wear slung over their shoulders. More than that, most *serapes* are sold for exorbitant prices to *gringos* who come down from the north.

Before I tell you about the circumstances of my purchase, let me furnish you with some insight into my background and needs. From the time I was a little boy, I can honestly say that I *never* wanted a *serape*. I never coveted, craved, or desired a *serape*. In my wildest fantasy, I never saw myself

with a *serape*. I could have lived my entire life without a
serape and looked back and said, "You know, it was a good
life." That being the case, how did this need—a need that
I never knew I had—develop and get satisfied?

Seven years ago, my wife and I went to Mexico City. We
were walking about, when she suddenly tugged my elbow
and said, "Hark! Yonder I see lights!" (She speaks that way,
you know.)

I grunted, "Oh no—I'm not going over there. That's the
crass commercial section for tourists. I didn't come all this
way for that. I came here to pick up the flavor of a different
culture . . . to encounter the unexpected . . . to get in touch
with unspoiled humanity . . . to experience the authentic . . .
to move through the streets with the ebb and flow. If you
want to wallow in commercialism, go ahead. I'll meet you
back at the hotel."

My wife, unconvinced and independent as always, waved
goodbye and left. Moving through the streets with the ebb and
flow, I noticed a genuine native some distance away. Approaching closer I saw that despite the heat, he was wearing
a *serape*. Actually, he was wearing a lot of *serapes* and
shouting, "Twelve hundred pesos!"

"Who can he be talking to?" I asked myself. "Surely not
me! In the first place, how could he know that I'm a tourist?
In the second place, I could not be cueing him, even sub-
liminally, that I want a *serape!*" As I mentioned earlier, I
absolutely did *not* want a *serape!*

Doing my best to ignore him, I picked up the pace somewhat. "Okay," he said. "I go from one thousand pesos and
give a bargain—eight hundred pesos."

At this point I spoke to him directly for the first time.
"My friend, I certainly respect your initiative, your diligence,
and your persistence. However, I do not *want* a *serape*. I do
not covet, crave, or desire this item. Would you kindly sell
your product elsewhere?" I even spoke to him in his own
language, "Do you understando?"

"*Sí,*" he replied, indicating he understood perfectly.

Again, I strode away, only to hear his footsteps behind me. Still with me, as if we were attached by a chain, he said over and over, "Eight hundred pesos!"

Somewhat annoyed, I started to jog, but the *serape* seller matched me stride for stride. He was now down to six hundred pesos. We had to stop at the corner for traffic, and he continued his one-way conversation, "Six hundred pesos! ... Five hundred pesos! ... All right, all right, four hundred pesos!"

When the traffic passed, I dashed across the street hoping he would be deterred. Before I even turned around, I heard his lumbering footsteps and his voice, "Señor, four hundred pesos!"

By now I was hot, sweating, tired, and irritated with his tenacity. Somewhat breathless, I confronted him. Spitting the words through half-clenched teeth I said, "Dammit, I just told you, I don't want a *serape*. Now stop following me!"

From my attitude and tone he seemed to get the message.

"Okay, you win," he repsonded. "*For you only,* two hundred pesos."

"What did you say?" I called out, surprised by my own words.

"Two hundred pesos!" he reiterated.

"Let me see one of those *serapes!*"

Why did I ask to see the *serape*? Did I need a *serape*? Did I want a *serape*? Did I even like a *serape*? No, I don't think so—but maybe I changed my mind.

Don't forget that this native serape seller started at twelve hundred pesos. He now wanted only two hundred pesos. I didn't even know what I was doing; yet somehow I had negotiated the price down one thousand pesos.

As we commenced our more formal negotiations, I found out from this merchant that the cheapest anyone ever paid for a *serape* in the history of Mexico City was a fellow from Winnipeg, Canada. He bought one for 175 pesos, but his mother and father were born in Guadalajara. Well, I got mine for 170 pesos, giving me the new *serape* record for Mexico City that I would take back to America for the Bicentennial year!

It was a hot day, and I was perspiring. Nevertheless, I was wearing my *serape* and feeling terrific. Adjusting it so it enhanced my body contours, modest as they are, I admired my reflected image in store fronts as I sauntered to the hotel.

Entering our room where my wife was stretched out on a bed reading a magazine I exulted, "Hey, look what I got!"

"What did you get?" she inquired.

"A beautiful *serape!*"

"What did you pay for it?" she asked casually.

"Let me put it this way," I said with confidence. "A native negotiator wanted twelve hundred pesos, but the international negotiator—who occasionally resides with you on weekends— bought it for 170 pesos."

She grinned. "Gee, that's interesting, because I got an identical one for 150 pesos. It's in the closet."

After my face fell, I checked the closet, removed my *serape*, and sat down to think about what had happened.

Why did I really buy that *serape?* Did I ever need a *serape?* Did I ever want a *serape?* Did I even like a *serape?* No, I don't think so. But on the streets of Mexico City I encountered not a peddler, but an international psychological negotiating marketeer. This individual constructed a process that met my particular needs. To be sure, he met needs that I didn't even know I had.

Obviously, I am not only talking about my *serape,* but somewhere in the back of a closet or high on a shelf, you may have acquired what I call a figurative *serape.* You know what I mean: The porcelain Canadian Mountie made in Hong Kong, the puka shell beads hand gathered on the island of Maui, the genuine Zuni ring, the piece of turquoise mined just west of Bisbee, the sparkling abalone shell, the Spanish doubloon washed ashore at Boca Raton, or the authentic Wells Fargo belt buckle.

To me, all these things are *"serapes"* and almost everyone I know has one. Think about your *serape* acquisition. Was it the item itself or the process that met your needs?

Basically, my message is simple. You can get what you want if you recognize that each person is unique and needs can be reconciled. At the same time, never forget that most needs can be fulfilled by the way you act and behave. Mutual satisfaction should be your goal and the means of achievement—collaborative Win-Win negotiations.

PART FOUR

NEGOTIATING ANYTHING, ANY PLACE

*He is free who knows how
to keep in his own hands
the power to decide.*
    —Salvador de Madariaga

10. Telephone negotiations and memos of agreement

The telephone is a vital verbal link in modern life. On a daily basis, you probably use a phone more often than you do a knife, fork, or spoon. A phone is attractively shaped. It's smooth to the touch. It's easy to pick up. It looks harmless. *Is* it harmless? No. It can cause serious misunderstandings ("I had no idea you meant *that!*"). It can be employed as an instrument of deception ("Your check is in the mail"). And it is a powerful economic force—millions of dollars are gained or lost according to the degree of understanding with which it is used.

Above all, the telephone commands attention. When its persistent ringing occurs, there is always the instinctive thought, "Who wants me?" Even would-be suicides have been lured from high, narrow ledges by the compelling need to answer its call.

Yet despite its significance, few people take the time to

examine the unique role the telephone plays in negotiations. Let us analyze this widespread activity.

Characteristics of Phone Negotiations:

1. More misunderstanding

Because visual feedback is lacking, it's easier to be misunderstood on the phone than in person. Talking to someone on the phone, you can't observe facial expressions and behavioral cues. The interpretation of voice tones is often faulty. Not only can voice tones be "misread," but innuendos and hidden meanings can be conjured up where none exist—or missed where they do exist.

2. Easier to say no

It's effortless and uncomplicated to say no on the phone. Let's assume I dial your number. I politely say, "I'd like you to do the following, if you don't mind . . ."

You briskly reply, "I can't. I'm awfully busy right now. Thanks for calling anyway." *Click.* Because we aren't face to face, you have no difficulty turning me down.

But if I see you in person, you can't get rid of me that easily. I walk into your office and gasp, "Please . . . I've come a long way! Oh, what a trip!"

Standing there, perspiring profusely, tears in my eyes, I beseech your favor. It is unlikely that you will deny me under these circumstances.

Feeling guilty that I traveled so far, you may worry about my physical and mental state. Naturally, you would like to resolve the matter without a fuss. All things considered, the odds are strong that you will go along with my request.

Any time an idea, proposal, or request calls for a change in the current handling of affairs, it requires a personal oral presentation. Documents, letters, and phone calls may precede or follow such a meeting, but they are not persuasive in themselves.

The message is simple: If you are serious about getting something you want, present it yourself—in person.

3. Much quicker

Telephone negotiations are always shorter than person-to-person dealings. This is true because the length of a face-to-face meeting must justify the time, travel, and expense invested.

Consider a hypothetical situation in which your child is having some difficulty in school. Should you call the teacher involved, the phone conversation might last five to ten minutes. However, if you took time from your busy schedule to go in person, the discussion could extend thirty minutes to an hour.

4. More competitive

Owing to the relative brevity of a phone transaction, there's often insufficient time to share information and experiences and to explore the satisfaction of mutual needs. This reality, combined with the formal nature of phone contacts, produces a climate in which competitive Win-Lose behavior flourishes.

On the phone, people tend to be impersonal and stick more to the point. Conversation is not spontaneous, and the governing rules and procedures are the focus of discussion. As a result, the side with the stronger case prevails.

Theoretically, if you are a competitive negotiator with more power, it would be to your advantage to resolve a dispute by telephone. Insisting that the negotiation be done this way is part of your strategy to win at my expense.

Not surprisingly, in this context, I desire an eyeball-to-eyeball meeting. Then you will see me, not as a statistical exception to a general rule, but as a flesh-and-blood human being. When negotiators see each other and get involved in the normal exchange of greetings, nods, smiles, and head scratching, it dilutes antagonism. Discussion is freer, and there's less time pressure and a better opportunity for a mutually beneficial outcome.

Before going any further, let me briefly mention a frustrating and difficult negotiation. As almost everyone knows, the telephone company can be a formidable adversary.

After receiving your monthly statement, you call the business office concerning an unusual charge of $72 for a call allegedly placed to Kuala Lumpur, Malaysia, from your phone. As an orphan, living alone, without friends, who never married and failed geography in public school, you plead not guilty.

Yet in trying to explain this injustice you are confronted with an immovable object in the form of a supervisor whose voice and self-confidence remind you of General Douglas MacArthur—in drag. After countless telephone conversations, even the innocent among us are inclined to capitulate. In large measure, the reasons for the lack of negotiation success in such a situation are the subject of this chapter. In essence, you are playing poker with a dealer named Lucky, who invented the game and is using his cards.

5. Greater risk

By its very nature, a negotiation via telephone is generally quicker and more competitive than a personal meeting. It follows that such a negotiation is likely to produce a winner and a loser.

Implicit in these observations is an axiom to remember: In any type of negotiation, quick is always synonymous with risk.

Whether a conflict is resolved by phone or even in person, undue haste puts one party in potential jeopardy.

Who takes the risk in a quick settlement? The person who is less prepared and cannot determine equity. Let's say that

I cannot ascertain, based upon my data and observation, that your proposal is fair. Instead, I must rely totally upon your representation. If you are a sincere, honest, and straightforward person, I will benefit from my faith in your integrity. But what if your display of decency and façade of fairness are illusory? What if underneath those reassuring words lurks a "Soviet-style slicker"? In this case, I will be brutalized and humiliated.

Therefore, if you are less prepared, cannot verify the statements made, and have no basis to trust the other person from past dealings, the general rule is to wait it out. Jumping into a muddy puddle makes it muddier. After it has had time to settle, you can see the bottom and know what you're getting into. More often than not, success comes to the negotiator with greater patience and staying power.

So if it might be a one-time transaction and you cannot determine equity, slow things down and drag your feet. The best thing to do, when you do not know what to do, is to do nothing. It is only good sense to act when it is to your advantage and to avoid acting if acting would be solely to the advantage of your adversary. Remember, power is never constant; the passage of time can cause your bargaining leverage to increase.

Sometimes a negotiator will want to push for prompt action. Let's assume that I am better prepared than you or can at least ascertain, based upon my data and observation, that this agreement will meet my needs. I need not rely upon your representations or even your integrity. Obviously, in this instance, I will "go quick" without incurring any unnecessary risk.

6. Advantage—caller

Telephone calls are made for many reasons and sometimes for no reason at all. Still, most experienced people recognize that the telephone can be used as a potential offensive or defensive weapon in the negotiation arsenal. Hence, an effec-

tive negotiator does not "take things as they come," but antici-
pates the effects of his action or inaction.

In any phone conversation, the person placing the call—the
caller—is in a privileged position. The recipient of an unexpected incoming call—the callee—is handicapped.

To begin with, assume that we are involved in a lengthy
and humdrum negotiation. As far you are concerned the
matter is on the back burner—in limbo. Unexpectedly, I
make an "impromptu" telephone call suggesting a proposition
that will settle things between us. It this an impulsive act on
my part or a premeditated tactic?

Chances are, this phone call was *not* made on the spur of
the moment. Before making it, I weighed the available
options: face-to-face talk, letter, telegram, use of a third-party
intermediary, telephone, or inaction. Presumably, I selected
the phone call, at this particular moment, because it best suits
my objective. Of course, I have prepared extensively. I am in
a quiet place, free from distraction. In front of me are twelve
sharpened pencils and six blank pads of paper. At my right is
an adding machine or a calculator. Behind me is a computer
affording instant access to data. I have an objective, a strategy,
and tactics in mind. Additionally, I have anticipated your
possible objections and have the answers and facts to overcome them. Basically, I'm rarin' to go!

Now, let's look at your predicament. Surprised by this
precipitous phone call, you are not prepared. You even have
to struggle to find the phone under the mounds of paper on
your desk. Ready reference material is not within reach. As
we talk you are distracted by people who approach with questions and by lights flashing on your phone receiver. Compli-
cating matters further, you can't find the secretary, you can't
find the file, and you can't even find a pencil or pen.

Under these conditions, you are speaking with me at
great risk. Because I am much better prepared, you defer to
my arguments and computations. If I am an altruistic, benev-

olent, wonderful person, I'll give you justice and mercy. If I'm a Soviet slicker, I'll cream you.

Despite the problems and drawbacks I've detailed, you're involved in a great many telephone negotiations. And I'm not referring to nine-to-five work calls alone. Anyone who tries to arrange a group picnic, maintain a relationship with family or friends, deal with telephone solicitors, or make wedding plans knows what I'm referring to. In fact, putting a wedding together is like plotting the D-Day invasion.

You negotiate over the phone with a vast assortment of people, from total strangers to loved ones. Even if the negotiating "event" doesn't occur on the phone (and it frequently does), the process stage does. Phrasing it another way, you do your preliminary maneuvering via the phone, whether you clinch the deal on the phone or in person. Since you do use the phone so much, you should make that electronic device work for you, not against you.

The following are some suggestions that can be effortlessly customized to help you achieve success:

1. Be the caller, not the callee

Try to initiate the vast majority of your calls in potential adversary situations. If someone phones you and you aren't prepared, say the equivalent of, "I'm sorry, but I have an important meeting to attend. I'm already late. What time would it be convenient for me to call back?"

You see, the instant you say something like, "I have something else on my schedule—I'll call you back!" you're no longer the callee. When you prepare yourself and *do* call back, you're the caller.

2. Plan and prepare

Before you take action, think through the result you want and make sure that the phone call is the best way to get it.

Decide whether you wish a no answer or a yes answer. Earlier, we indicated that it is easier to get a no than a yes via telephone.

Someone once said, "If you fail to plan, you are planning to fail." Always think in terms of the specific objective or goal that you want achieved by the phone call. As the Koran says, "If you don't know where you are going, any road will get you there." Admittedly, if you don't know where you are going, you can never get lost. In the end, if you don't know where you are going, when you get there, you don't even know you're there!

The point is, as the caller, plan and prepare to make what you want happen. Here are a few tips for phone negotiations:

A. Prepare a checklist of points to be covered during the call.

B. Dry run the negotiation or transaction in your mind.

C. In an adversary encounter, attempt to anticipate the tactics of the other party. It is a truism that forewarned is forearmed.

D. Try to have all the relevant facts at hand as you make the phone call.

E. Notwithstanding your preparation, you may be surprised by diversions or off-the-cuff queries. Certainly, there is no indignity in admitting some lack of knowledge.

F. Concentrate and avoid distractions. Give this phone call your undivided attention. Don't be a contortionist. (This is the person who, while speaking or listening, performs other functions, from housekeeping to chatting with others.)

G. If facts and figures are involved, keep all reference material, plus an adding machine or pocket calculator, within arm's reach.

H. At the end, summarize what was agreed upon and define the responsibility for follow-up action.

3. A graceful exit

Always have a ready excuse to get off the phone if the discussion drifts in a direction detrimental to you. If a long-winded caller or Soviet slicker will not allow you to make a graceful exit, you can exercise the option of hanging up on *yourself*. *Please*—I would never recommend that you hang up on another person. That would be discourteous and socially unacceptable. Hang up while *you* are talking.

How can you convincingly hang up on yourself? Very simple. Say the equivalent of, "Hey, I'm really glad you called. You know, I was just thinking about you yester——" *Click*.

The other party will never assume that you hung up on yourself. He'll think the telephone company goofed again!

What's the upshot? The other party will call you back. When he does, you've just stepped out, if you're at the office, or you temporarily don't answer, if you're at home ("I had to get something from the garage"). This gives you time in which to prepare yourself so you will not be at the mercy of an unexpected call*er*.

4. Discipline yourself to listen

Effective listening requires more than hearing the words transmitted. It demands that you find meaning and understanding in what is being said. After all, "meanings are not in words, but in people."

Obviously, you can't listen intelligently while you are talking, so be sensitive to your own "listen-versus-talk ratio." Consider the use of the pregnant pause. This is a magical moment when you go mute. As soon as there's a prolonged silence on the line—especially during a long-distance call—the other party may talk compulsively, either out of nervousness or from a need to get his money's worth. Invariably, he will rephrase questions in a way that will give you valuable information.

5. Write the memorandum of agreement

"The horror of that moment," the King went on, "I shall never, *never* forget!"

"You will, though," the Queen said, "if you don't make a memorandum of it."

—Lewis Carroll

In the main, I'm not an advocate of written correspondence, memorandums, or notes. All things considered, memo mania infects our society to such an extent that proliferating paperwork clogs organizational arteries. From my viewpoint, most written documents are either unnecessary or unintelligible. Besides, writing everything down is time consuming, and most of us find it difficult.

Recognizing the arduous and wearisome nature of writing, Stephen Leacock, a professional author, said, "Writing is not hard. Just get paper and pencil, sit down, and write it as it occurs to you. The writing is easy—it's the occurring that's hard."

By and large, a good general rule is to avoid formal written communication where possible. Admittedly, there are times when you must take pen in hand. On these occasions it is advisable to remember: Whatever you put down on paper should be written as if it will ultimately be read in a court of law.

Implicit in the phrase "general rule" is that there's an exception. Naturally, there is, in the case of a memorandum of agreement. This is the document that you compose after the resolution of a conflict or dispute. It sets forth the commitments of each party that form the basis of the settlement.

After you've finished an *important* telephone transaction, carefully compose this written representation of the negotiated understanding. Inform the other person, while still on the phone, that you're going to do so. You should write such a memorandum after any significant face-to-face agreement as well.

Experience has shown that a gentleman's agreement can become very ungentlemanly. As Sam Goldwyn is purported to have said, "A verbal agreement isn't worth the paper it's written on."

The memorandum of agreement is sometimes called a letter of intent or a memo of understanding. Whatever name is used, the purpose is the same: to define the commitments of the parties involved. Typically, they are written in moth-eaten language as if the writer used a quill pen. Some of these documents are so stilted and pompous that you might think the composer wears high-button shoes and celluloid collars. Here's the way they generally read:

"Pursuant to our conversation on such-and-such a date, we have agreed to the following. . . ."

"As per our telephone dialogue, we have concluded that . . ."

"In reference to the matter of . . ."

"Acknowledging our phone conversation of . . ."

Actually, the format is usually not important. What is crucial is that *you* do the writing. Why should you undertake this burden? Because the advantages to you are enormous.

What are the scribe's benefits?

A. You have the initiative, determining when the memo will be written, the form it will take, and when it will be dispatched. Nothing will happen until you make it happen!

B. The agreement will be expressed in your terms. If there's any question about interpretation, we always ask the person who composed the document. For example, if a letter written by James Madison regarding school busing or abortion were discovered behind a desk drawer, these dilemmas could be resolved quickly. After all, who knows better than the author how the Constitution should be interpreted?

Let's refocus from a phone transaction to a face-to-face transaction. I'm your adversary seated across from you at a rectangular conference table. The negotiating sessions go on and on, day after day.

Am I taking notes? No. Like many top executives, I falsely think I have a photographic mind. Are you taking notes? You can bet your bottom dollar you are. Why are you taking notes? Because doing so may give you leverage and power with respect to me.

After the third day, I irritatedly ask you, during a break, "Why are you taking so *many* notes? You aren't a court reporter! We've already *covered* those aspects of the proposed contract like a tent!"

You smile, shrug, and mumble something about not being able to remember anything without committing it to paper.

On the fifth day, my photographic mind isn't as photographic as I thought. During another break, I pull you aside and ask, "Tell me—what did we say about those three new codicils to the contract? They aren't quite clear to me, especially since we added two other codicils on Tuesday. I'm afraid I'm getting them mixed up!"

You thumb through your notes while I impatiently tap my foot. "Here it is . . . the three new codicils were spelled out on Wednesday at 2:00 P.M."

I study your scrawling. I frown at your hieroglyphics. "I can't make heads or tails of your handwriting!"

In the manner of a fighter pilot recapping a combat mission, you reply, "The codicils were so-and-so, and so-and-so, and so-and-so."

I make a face. "All I see on that page is two dots, an asterisk, and a star!"

You give me your best choir-boy look. "That's what those marks *mean!*"

Suddenly, I regard you with awe. You now have considerable power. Who can better interpret the chicken scratches than the chicken that scratched them?

C. When you know from the outset that you will be writing the memo of agreement, you listen more effectively and take better notes. Indeed, you will be more attentive and exercise considerable self-discipline.

D. Your initial draft will establish the framework for any possible future revisions. It will determine definitions and set the limits for discussion.

Here's an example. Let's say you and I wrap up a phone transaction. You agree to let me write the letter of intent, without realizing the effects of your gesture. I write the memo and mail you a copy.

Two days later, you phone me and say, "Hey, wait a minute! I got your write-up, and you left out item A."

"Item A?" I reply, all innocence.

"Yeah," you continue. "Remember A?"

I act slightly puzzled. "Oh . . . item A. I seem to remember your mentioning it briefly."

You persist, "Well, why didn't you put it in?"

I counter with, "I didn't think it was that important. After all, you hardly mentioned it."

You clear your throat. "I hardly mentioned it because you seemed to agree with it."

I pause for a moment, as though you're imposing on me —as though you're asking for too much. Then I say, "Do you really want it in?"

You reply, "Yes, I really want it in."

I pause again. "Well, why don't we just have a private understanding that it's in there, even though it isn't?"

You get irritated. "No—I want it in!"

Why am I giving you such a rough time regarding A? Assume that I'm a collaborative negotiator, how could A be left out? Some selectivity always occurs in producing any writing. Otherwise, the agreement would be the size of *War and Peace*. But if I write the agreement any selectivity will be at your expense. The items that are somehow important to me are included. But it's hard for me to read your mind. Remember, you hardly mentioned A during the negotiation.

Ultimately, I will give you item A. Please note, though, that I have made a concession to you on this point and now expect something in return. Furthermore, after such a difficult time with A, you may be hesitant to ask about item B, which I also left out of the draft. Your attitude now is, "Brother, I'm not going through all that hassle again!"

And so, the power of the scribe prevails again.

E. Because you've bothered to do the writing, the other party is appreciative. They tend not to be picayune or quibble over lesser points. Even if your write-up contains some minor imperfections, most people will be magnanimous and not engage in hair splitting.

In conclusion, let me summarize with a pithy comment of Ellen Eisenstadt. When her boss gave her a pat on the back and a vague promise of future opportunities, she remarked, "The pen is mightier than a pat and a promise."

Why should I question the monkey
when I can question the organ grinder?
　　　　　　　　—Aneurin Bevan

11. Moving up

Does the squeaky wheel *really* get the grease? Yes—if it knows where and how to squeak.

Let's cover a grievance that you may have against a large, seemingly impersonal bureaucracy. I recommend . . .

1. Phone the organization's nearest office. Get the full name and position of the person you speak with. Put your plight in simple human terms so they can identify with you. After asking for their help, obtain a verbal commitment and a time for remedial action to occur.
2. Follow up the phone call with a gracious letter to remind the person with whom you spoke that you are counting on them.
3. Just before the action deadline, call your "friend" to check on the progress of their personal efforts. If this doesn't stir things up . . .
4. Visit the nearest office in person. Be polite and courteous. See your "friend," but make sure others are also

aware of the injustice that still exists. Solicit help from
others so they feel an obligation to assist in finding
an equitable solution.

What if the preceding still doesn't result in satisfactory
action? *Move up another level.* Every organization is a hierarchy. Steadily go up the ladder, rung by rung, until you *get*
satisfaction. The higher you go, the more likely you are to
have your needs met.

Why? Several reasons. People who are higher up understand
that general rules were never meant to cover every specific
situation. They're more aware of the Big Picture and can
visualize the fall-out that might result from improper handling.
Even more significant, they have greater authority and get
paid to take some risks and make decisions.

At any level, try not to negotiate with a person who lacks
authority, unless you enjoy wasting your time. If you're
considering interacting with someone, first ask yourself: Who
is this individual? What experience have others had with
him? Where is he on the organizational chart? What types of
decisions can he actually make? Does he have any real clout?

When you've determined all this to a reasonable extent,
check it out by asking the person, politely but pointblank,
"Can you remedy this situation?" or, "Are you able to help
me solve this problem?" or, "Do you have the authority to
take the kind of action I want right now?" If the response is
negative, turn to someone else.

No one has total authority, so don't expect it. All you
can expect of someone with moderate to considerable authority
—especially in a bureaucracy—is that if he makes an agreement, he'll do everything in his power to implement it. He'll
crawl out on a limb to honor his commitment. He'll stick
his neck out for you, if only because it's a matter of his
integrity and principle.

When Menachem Begin of Israel finally agreed to go along
with the Mideast peace formula, he said the equivalent of this

to President Carter: "I don't have the authority to make a definite national commitment, but I will guarantee that if the Israeli Parliament doesn't ratify the agreement, I'll resign." You can't ask for more than that.

Let me give you five examples of a squeaky wheel getting the grease because it moves up to levels of greater authority. In each case, you're the hypothetical squeaky wheel.

Here's the first example. Because the plane you took dragged its wings in a holding pattern, thanks to a thunderstorm, you arrive at a hotel forty minutes before midnight. Your suit is damp and wrinkled, your shoes are wet, you have dyspepsia, and you're fatigued right down to your bone marrow. Even your teeth are tired. You're eager to hit the sack in that single room for which you have a guaranteed reservation. Thank God you have that reservation.

The check-in clerk glances at you, then mutters, in a flat, metallic voice, "Yes, your reservation *is* guaranteed, but we don't have a room. We accidentally overbooked. It happens once in a while."

What should you do? Immediately lower your suitcase to the carpet and remind yourself that the clerk is, at that moment, basically a reacting, nonthinking machine. He's behaving like a programmed robot or computer, feeding you information his superiors in the hotel's hierarchy fed to him. They told him there are no rooms available. Parrotlike, he's transmitting this data to you. Since he isn't thinking of options at the hotel's disposal, it's up to you to help him solve *their* problem.

You run the options through your head. The hotel may have a suite it can give you. It can put a bed in one of its meeting rooms. It might let you use the living room portion of a suite. It could even have a room, if you intend to leave early the next morning.

As a starter you say, "Well . . . how about a suite? How about the Governor's Suite, if the others are taken? I know you have meeting rooms and conference rooms. They're advertised in all your brochures. Could you put a bed in one of the conference rooms or meeting rooms?"

The clerk balks. "Oh, no—we can't do anything like that. Why don't you let me try to put you up in another hotel?"

You reply, "I don't *want* to be put up in another hotel. I'm tired, and I want to go to bed, to quote an old song. And I want to go to bed right here. Let me talk to your general manager, please." (You know the general manager won't be on duty this late at night, but you want the clerk to know you are determined.)

The clerk makes a face, picks up a special phone, and mumbles something into its mouthpiece. The *night* manager suddenly appears, as you knew he would. You repeat your query about suites, meeting rooms, and other available options.

The night manager consults a room chart, frowns, and looks up. "We *do* happen to have a suite left. It's being re- decorated. However, it's double the price of a single room."

You quietly but firmly state, "It *shouldn't* cost one red cent more, because I have a guaranteed reservation!"

The night manager sighs, then says, "Well . . . do you want it or not?"

You reply, "I'll take it . . . and we'll discuss the price tomorrow."

Next morning, when you're at the front counter again, ready to check out, you're presented with your bill. Sure enough, it's double the price you expected to pay. *Now* you ask to see the general manager. Are you self-confident? Yes. You know you're in the driver's seat, because the service has already been rendered. (Once a service has been rendered, it's never as valuable as it was prior to being rendered.) You in- form the general manager about your surprise when the hotel failed to honor its reservations policy. After listening to his explanation, you now discuss the exorbitant room charge.

Ninety-five percent of the time, the general manager will apologize for the billing error. He'll let you pay the single- room price for the suite. He knows that, had it not been for the hotel's carelessness, the question of the room charge would never have come up. And he's aware that in the long run, it pays to be fair.

Let me give you a personal "for instance" involving a similar situation. Two years ago, I had a guaranteed reservation at a Manhattan hotel. As I took a taxi to my destination, late in the evening, the driver said, "We'll have to stop at this corner. The street's blocked. It looks like a police barricade."

"Oh, great," I grumbled, getting out of the cab and paying my fare. Hoisting my bags, I shouldered my way past policemen, press photographers, gawking pedestrians, TV camera crews, and newspaper personnel.

"Hey, what's going on?" I asked the doorman, after trudging to the hotel's ornate entranceway.

He pointed skyward. "Some guy on the eleventh floor's about to jump. That's what's going on!"

"Gee, that's too bad," I said, upset at the thought of a fellow human tumbling to the sidewalk. I edged through the revolving door and approached the desk. "My name's Cohen," I said. "Herbert A. Cohen. I have a guaranteed reservation."

The registration clerk murmured, "Yes, you do, Mr. Cohen ... but we don't have a room."

I grimaced. "What do you *mean,* you don't have a room?"

"Sorry," said the clerk, "but we're all filled up. You know how it is."

"No, I *don't* know how it is!" I retorted. "You *have* to have a room somewhere!"

"Let me check around at other hotels," he suggested, reaching for a desk phone.

"Hold it!" I snapped. "You *do* have a room! You know the guy on the eleventh floor? The one who's causing all that commotion outside? *He's checking out!*"

The wind-up? The guy didn't jump. The police corralled him but checked him into a different facility for psychiatric examination. I got his vacant room.

Let me give you another personal experience. In the winter of 1978, I flew to Mexico City to conduct a negotiations seminar for local businessmen. I had a reservation at a magnificent hotel. Unfortunately, the hotel could not honor it. The registration clerk announced that all rooms were filled. Apparently, guests had stayed over because a snowstorm had canceled flights to the Midwestern United States.

After making no progress with the clerk, primarily because of a language problem, I asked to see the manager. I lit a cigar, rested an elbow on the marble check-in counter, and asked the manager, "What if the president of Mexico showed up? Would you have a room for him?"

"Sí señor . . ."

I blew a smoke ring toward the ceiling. "Well, he's not coming, so I'll take his room."

Did I get a room? You bet, but I had to promise that if the president arrived, I would vacate immediately.

Here's the second "moving up" example. You and your daughter shop for an evening gown for her high school senior prom. She finds one that thrills her to the bottom of her feet. You purchase it and take it home, and your daughter promptly comes down with a severe case of stomach flu. With tears in her eyes, she calls her date from a bedside phone and informs him she'll have to cancel.

"What about the evening gown?" you ask, displaying poor timing and a poor sense of priorities.

"Please take it back!" she sobs, burying her face in a pillow. "I never want to see it again. I *hate* it!"

You return the evening gown to the dress shop.

"I'm very sorry," mumurs a clerk, "but we have a no-returns policy."

"She didn't even wear the dress!" you protest. "The price tag's still on it!"

You glance at a wall sign. It states: NO RETURNS (the power of legitimacy).

"I want to talk to the proprietor!" you say.

"She's out to lunch. Won't be back for forty-five minutes."

"I'll wait," you mumble, seating yourself on the nearest chair. (If you can't get satisfaction from someone, go over that person's head. Move up a level.)

In forty-five minutes, the proprietor returns. You closet yourself with her in her office. You explain the circumstances: Your daughter's sick; the gown was never worn.

"How do I know the gown wasn't worn?" the proprietor asks. "This is an old trick some parents pull. They simply reattach the price tag, then try to remove any soiled spots with a damp rag!"

You show her the purchase date on the sales slip. You offer to phone your family physician, in her presence, to verify that your daughter was home ill the night of the prom.

"Oh, all right," concedes the proprietor. "We'll make an exception this time. I'll have the woman who waited on you cancel the charge for the gown."

You see, there's an exception to every rule. Rules are general. In most cases, they should be adhered to, or we'd live in a world of anarchy. But let me give you one simplistic example where a rule *should* be broken.

You're listening to a sermon in church. The congregation is silent, hanging on the minister's every word. There's a rule in that church that no one speaks during a sermon. To speak would break the spell. Suddenly, you detect a flicker of flame at the base of one wall. A wire behind the plaster is malfunctioning. What should you do? If you cannot break a rule under any circumstances, you have three alternatives.

1. Cue the minister by blowing the smoke his way.
2. Compose a note that will be passed slowly down to the pulpit, reading, "The church is on fire!"
3. Get up and leave without a word, since there's no rule against this behavior.

The particular circumstances govern whether or not you can justifiably break a reasonable rule. If you do not want a policy or regulation to govern your situation, be prepared to demonstrate that the framers of this rule never intended it to cover your unique facts.

Here's the third "moving up" example. You dutifully mail in your federal tax form by midnight, April 15. You've answered every question like an Eagle Scout, falsifying nothing. Two months later, you receive a modified form letter from the Internal Revenue Service. The IRS wants you to visit a local office at 10:00 A.M. the following Thursday. There are discrepancies that need straightening out.

Your stomach wraps around your spine. You idiotically fantasize that you *must* be guilty of *something*.

Use your head. Stop being emotional. Let your stomach relax. No one's going to flog you with a truncheon. In actuality, you'll be treated with exaggerated respect. You'll get the "kid glove treatment."

Carrying pertinent records and canceled checks, you drop by the IRS office at 10:00 A.M., per instructions. You tell the receptionist your name, then glance over his left shoulder. Rows of desks pop into focus behind him. Seated at each desk is an individual with an electronic calculator, a pad of paper, tax-table books, and a serious, kindly face. Remember four things about these auditors:

1. They're simply doing a job . . . and not making much money at it.
2. They dislike paying taxes as much as you do. When it comes to their own taxes, they probably fudge a trifle to the same extent as the general populace. In fact, some of *them* are also audited.
3. If not very imaginative, they tend to "go by the book," thinking in general terms, rather than specific applications.

   And here's the biggie:
4. Despite electronic claculators, what they do is subjective and evaluative. It's anything but objective, air-

tight, and fool-proof. In brief, *your interpretations and evaluations may be as valid as theirs*. If you doubt this, consider the well-publicized instances, each year, in which ear-marked returns have been shuttled past eight to ten auditors. Have the "test" auditors, stirring the same broth, cooked up the same figures? No. The figures have been unbelievably—almost laughably—divergent.

As you wait for your name to be called, you double-check what you're wearing to make sure you aren't overdressed.

You should never dress like a fashion plate when entering an IRS office. Don't look like a bum, but also don't resemble the front cover of *Gentlemen's Quarterly* or *Harper's Bazaar*. The person you deal with will feel comfortable with you, and friendly toward you, only if he or she can identify with you. (This is a psychological insight sharp trial lawyers cash in on so they won't turn juries off. Some leave their hair in need of a trim; others don't shave too closely; and still others let their shoes get scuffy.)

Your name is called. Simultaneously, a designated auditor steps forward to greet you. At this point—and throughout the transaction—your attitude is one of pure "Help me!" You personalize yourself, coming across as a reasonable, likable, friendly human being. Are you argumentative? To the contrary. Are you defensive? Absolutely not. You're there to be cooperative. Butter wouldn't melt in your mouth.

The auditor says, "There are four things I want to discuss with you: first, your charitable contributions; second, the figure you put down for home depreciation; third, your enhancement of your property through extensive additions; and fourth, the amount of money you claim you sent in as a quarterly tax payment."

You clear your throat. This may be tougher than you anticipated. But *need* it be? No. Just play it cool.

The auditor continues, "I'd like to see verification of the

$900.00 you put down on your return for charitable contributions."

"No problem," you reply. "I have the canceled checks right here, in this envelope."

The auditor thumbs through the checks, concurrently depressing buttons on the desk-top calculator. "These only total $360.00. How do you account for the other $540.00?"

Your answer is as sincere as it is quick. "I faithfully go to church every Sunday. Each time, I drop ten dollars in the collection plate."

"Fifty-two times a year?"

"Without fail. That comes to five hundred dollars."

"What about the remaining forty dollars?"

You don't even bother to clear your throat. "That was for Girl Scout cookies, hand-outs to kids soliciting funds for Little League Baseball, and so forth. I probably should have put down sixty bucks for all that."

"Hmmm . . ." comments the auditor. "That's hard to believe. No one's that generous!"

You shrug. "I am."

"I'm going to put a question mark next to that $540.00 figure," says the auditor.

Note the situation here. The auditor can't prove that you *didn't* drop ten dollars in the plate each Sunday or dispense money to fresh-faced youngsters. That's strictly a matter of judgment of what is reasonable. With respect to matters of judgment, the IRS doesn't have you "dead to rights," as the saying goes. There can always be an appeal to a higher level.

The interaction continues. The auditor claims your home-depreciation figure should reflect a twelve-year period. You politely disagree, reiterating that the figure should reflect an eight-year period. You stick to your guns, like Stonewall Jackson at the Battle of Bull Run. Nothing can budge you. Does the IRS have you dead to rights? No. This, too, is a matter of judgment. This, too, can be appealed.

Having scrawled a second question mark with a Magic

Marker, the auditor, a literalist from the word "go," proceeds. "You enhanced your property by $2,000.00 when you made the additions spelled out on page four of the typewritten sheets attached."

"Oh, no—you have that all wrong," you state quietly. "Those weren't additions. They were badly needed repairs. The house was falling apart. You should have seen it! If I hadn't done what I did, it would have resembled a tarpaper shack!"

The auditor smiles wryly, as though suffering from a gas pain. Even a literalist can have a sense of humor. This is another matter of judgment. Therefore, another question mark is scrawled. You now have a third matter that can be moved up the pyramid.

You come a cropper on the fourth point of contention. You claim, on your tax return, that you paid $1,400.00 in quarterly tax payments. The IRS has proof that you paid only $900.00. The figure you put down was a slip-up—an honest mistake on your part. You filled out the form late at night, and your mind was tired. Here the IRS *does* have you dead to rights. It's not a matter of judgment. There's no chance to appeal. You must make up the $500.00 difference.

But what if the auditor disagrees with you on those *other* points: your charitable contributions, home depreciation, and property enhancement?

The answer is simple. If you acted honestly and believe you are right, start moving up. *Appeal.* First, make an appointment with an IRS examiner. If that get-together doesn't satisfy you, make an appointment with a member of the Office of the Regional Director of Appeals. If *that* get-together doesn't satisfy you, take your case to court—either a United States tax court, a United States court of claims, or a United States district court. In short, even if only a small amount is involved, appeal, if you're so inclined. You have Constitutional rights. Lean on them. You also have guts. Use them.

One final note about negotiating with the IRS: If various

auditors and examiners demand that you produce additional verification for everything, as if you were a magician who can yank rabbits from hats, don't rush. Get delays. Tell whomever you're dealing with that it's going to take a *long, long* time to run down the required records. Use time, and learn to live with the ambiguity, because it will save you money in the long run.

Remember, the IRS is eager to close your file. Fencing with you requires people, time, and money. The effort expended on your case produces a very poor return, and they know it. So continue to say, "Look, I'm sure I'm right. Perhaps we can work something out." Eventually, even when it believes it's right, the IRS is willing to negotiate matters of this type. As you move up you will find more understanding for your point of view. The higher-ups know that sound tax administration requires flexibility in dealing with questions of judgment about trivial sums.

Here's the fourth "moving up" example. You and a friend decide to rent a rustic summer cottage for weekend use, sixty miles from the city in which you live. When you arrive, the first weekend, you discover that the cottage needs an incredible amount of repair work. The doors don't open and close properly, the plumbing is faulty, much of the wiring demands attention, and the kitchen range is a disaster area. Fortunately, you're clever with your hands. Unfortunately, you haven't brought tools, parts, or very much money with you.

Leaving your companion to sweep floors and wash windows, you drive to a nearby town and enter a convenient hardware store. After an hour of searching, you find all the parts you need, plus the tools required to attach and fit them where they belong. The shopping cart you've been wheeling up and down the aisles is full. You push it to a check-out counter, and the clerk at the cash register rings up the total of $84.00.

"Eight-four dollars!" you exclaim. "That's unbelievable! I'll have to write out a check."

"Sorry," says the clerk. "This store doesn't accept checks."

Let's freeze the frame. Why doesn't this hardware store accept checks? At one time it did, but it was burned. Three percent of the checks it received bounced. Universalizing from that three percent, the proprietor adopted a new store policy. Frowning like Scrooge, he proclaimed to those at the cash registers, "Don't accept checks, ever!" That's why the clerks at the cash registers unthinkingly obey this iron-clad rule, making no exceptions.

And then you show up. "You *have* to accept my check," you state. "Otherwise, I won't be able to move into the cottage I've rented."

"Sorry," repeats the clerk. "I have my orders."

"Who *gave* you those orders?" you ask.

"The owner," he replies.

"I want to speak to him," you say.

The proprietor appears. "What's the story?" he asks.

"I need these tools and parts," you answer, "and your clerk won't accept a check."

He stares at the shopping cart. "How much does all that come to?"

"Eighty-four dollars," you reply.

"You don't have the cash?" he asks.

"No, but my credit's first-rate. I bank at the State National in Middletown."

Let's stop the action again. Are you in a good bargaining position, despite store policy? Yes. The best time to negotiate for acceptance of a check is after you've used a store's services. The proprietor is staring at the eighty-four dollars' worth of parts and tools in your shopping cart. He's thinking, "Oh, my God, if this meatball says, 'Forget it!' and walks out the front door in a huff, I have to take all these items, one by one, and put them back on the shelves. That'll take forever!"

Will he accept your check? Yes, if you show him proper identification, then give him your bank's phone number, as well as the phone number of the outfit you work for. Remember: In most instances, an order-enforcing subordinate is simply a mouthpiece, acting in a robotlike manner. Sidestep robots. Negate any policy that's detrimental to your interests by taking a step upward. The person who gives the policy can also take it away. Afford law givers a chance to amend their policy in light of your particular situation. Often, they are grateful for this opportunity.

Here's the fifth "moving up" example. Your youngest son, who's in seventh grade, is having a terrible time with mathematics. It isn't that he's not bright: He's a crackerjack at English. But he can't seem to grasp anything quantifiable. Why? His mathematics teacher humiliated him in front of classmates because he failed to show up for special help after school when ordered to do so. Now he has a mental block regarding numbers. That's bad enough. What's worse is that if this teacher doesn't give him a begrudging nod, your son won't advance into eighth grade. The boy's hypersensitive. It would wipe out his psyche.

How do you negotiate your kid into eighth grade? Obviously, I am assuming that this outcome is just and beneficial to all parties concerned. It's crucial that you confront the math teacher before he actually gives and records the flunking grade. for the year.

Once a grade is on the school's records, it's almost set in concrete, so to speak. This presupposes that your child confides in you regarding his predicament. You *must* have a good relationship with your offspring—a relationship of mutual trust, based on acceptance of each other's shortcomings.

It's also crucial that you see the math teacher in person. Don't negotiate with him on the phone. Saying no on the phone is easy. Being unreasonable on the phone is easy. Saying no and being unreasonable face to face is something else again.

When you huddle with the teacher, personalize like mad. Make sure he favorably perceives you, and your needs, with every one of his nerve endings. If that doesn't work, immediately appeal to the next level in the school system's hierarchy. Keep climbing the ladder, if need be, till you closet yourself with the superintendent of schools.

Normally, the superintendent of schools will be much more understanding of the stalemate than will the math teacher. Why? Because the superintendent is intensely political. He or she perceives you, not only as a complaining, concerned parent, but as a taxpayer—a taxpayer who can address the school board at its next meeting, along with fellow disgruntled parents, and initiate a mass movement to reduce school taxes.

That remote possibility, and the possibility of concurrent negative publicity, makes the superintendent shudder.

Will your son pass into eighth grade? Yes—if you move fast. The higher you go in any administrative pyramid, the better off you are. Those in the rarefied air of the higher altitudes are more flexible and pragmatic than those at the bottom of the pyramid. They're more willing to flex so-called unbendable rules.

A final word about moving up. In most sizable communities, there are all sorts of people and groups you can appeal to for help, such as the Better Business Bureau, the Chamber of Commerce, consumer groups, Call for Action operations on TV or in the newspapers, and even legislators. Don't hesitate to plug in to such facilities. To quote Hubert Humphrey on the subject of principle: "Never give up and never give in."

To resort to power one need not be violent,
and to speak to conscience one need not be
meek. The most effective action both
resorts to power and engages conscience.
>   —Barbara Deming

12. Taking it personally

Within our own lifetimes, the accelerating pace of change and the increasing complexity of problems stagger even the experts. All organizations have grown—larger and away from us. As a result, some people feel like strangers, like ciphers lost in the crowd. Such an attitude is a curious blend of apathy and despair. The apt metaphor is Franz Kafka's *The Castle,* with its red tape and faceless masses waiting in endless lines.

It's as if we have become depersonalized, like minute particles of some great statistical census—working ants in the giant anthill of life.

But it wasn't always this way. You may recall a time when, even in a large city, people went into a neighborhood store and the owner greeted them by name. Although this way of doing business may have been less efficient than modern commerce, it was somehow more satisfying.

Obviously, I am not advocating that we "return to those thrilling days of yesteryear." What I am suggesting is that if you are to negotiate effectively, the other party must not see you as a statistic, a thing, a commodity, or an article of commerce. If you present yourself as a unique, vulnerable human being, there is greater likelihood that you will get what you want. How many of us can be indifferent to those we see in human terms without being indifferent to ourselves? Deep down, most people know that their own welfare is related to the welfare of others. Any slight to my neighbor eventually becomes an injury to myself.

Theoretically, we may know that "no man is an island," but faced with the pressures of daily living, we tend to forget this interdependence. Therefore, it's up to you to humanize yourself so that you are not seen as a depersonalized statistic. No one identifies with large numbers, but almost everyone commiserates with the anguish of a flesh-and-blood person.

This fact is implicit in the reputed comment of Samuel Adams, just prior to the American Revolution. During the planning of the Boston Massacre, Adams was reported to have said something to this effect: "There ought to be no fewer than three or four killed so we will have martyrs for the Revolution. However, there should be no more than twenty, because once you get beyond that number we no longer have martyrs, but simply a sewage problem."

Aside from Adams's callous remarks and their ethical implications, his theory was correct. To maximize the impact of an event, people must be able to indentify with those involved and with the circumstances.

When the Second World War was over, we learned the statistical magnitude of the atrocities committed against humankind. We could not fathom the absolute evil perpetrated by the Nazis and their countless millions of silent and passive accomplices. For the average person, the numbers were incomprehensible.

More than anything else, it was the writings of a teenage Jewish girl that helped people understand some of the horror that had taken place. While hiding from the Nazis, she wrote a vivid and tender account of her experiences. Her words expressed innocence, optimism, and humanity that produced an emotional impact. This was, of course, *Anne Frank: Diary of a Young Girl*, published in 1947 and later made into a play and a film that affected the world.

Accordingly, to maximize your impact as a negotiator—no matter whom you are dealing with—you must *personalize* both yourself and the situation.

How do you personalize yourself? You make the other party see you as a unique, flesh-and-blood, three-dimensional individual, someone who has feelings and needs, someone the other person likes, cares about, and somehow feels obligated to—at least someone the other person wants to do something for.

How do you personalize the situation? The answer is simple. Try not to negotiate on behalf of an institution or organization, no matter how large or small. Negotiate on behalf of *yourself, representing* the institution.

Let me elaborate. Few of us keep commitments to sterile institutions. They are too remote, lifeless, and abstract to create a sense of obligation or concern. No one, except an architect, cares a hoot about bricks, glass, steel, and concrete. Institutions are cold and lifeless. That's why IBM, Con Edison, General Electric, Ma Bell, the IRS, and other abstract entities get zapped so often. (Typical attitude: "What's the difference if the Mobil Oil Corporation loses $100,000? It's not even half a cent a share!") That's why it's self-defeating to negotiate on behalf of prosperous organizations, and obviously, that's why phrases like the following usually fall on their faces:

"On behalf of the Bensonhurst Chamber of Commerce we'd like you to . . ."

"For the benefit of the Boy Scouts of America, we want you to . . ."

"The Missouri Synod of the Lutheran Church urges you to . . ."

"For the sake of financial solvency, the National Organization of Women requests that you fulfill your pledge."

So if you represent the March of Dimes, the state of California, the United Way, the local women's club, the New York City Transit Authority, or what have you, and you're supposed to gain the commitment of others to these impersonal entities *per se* (virtually an impossibility), what can you do? You can personalize. You can gain the commitment of others to *you*.

Here's what I mean. Let's say you're with an organization, and someone you're negotiating with is giving you a hard time. Persuade that person to be concerned about you, not the institution, or to be concerned about you *via* the institution. Say the equivalent of:

"I happen to be with so-and-so . . . but didn't you promise me you were going to do this? I was counting on you. I assured my boss about it. I told my family. I guaranteed the auditor. You aren't going to let me down, are you?"

When the other party asks, "You aren't taking this personally, are you?" you plaintively reply, "Yes!"

In other words, "lay it on" the other party. Get him or her emotionally involved. It's difficult for people to back off if you say the equivalent of, "I'd appreciate it if you'd do this as a favor to me." Such phrases are extremely effective in personalizing situations. Of course, if you create an obligation on your part, it's understood that you'll reciprocate in kind when appropriate occasions arise.

This leads to the next question: How can you personalize *yourself* in some of your negotiation encounters?

Following are some down-to-earth illustrations:

Here's the first example. Let's say you're driving forty-five miles an hour in a thirty-five-mile zone. A squad car, concealed in a shrub-lined driveway, bags you on its radar. A siren blares as it trails you in merciless pursuit. You curb your auto, muttering because of the inconvenience. A cop steps from the squad car, then ambles toward you, ticket pad in hand, eyes unreadable behind one-way-mirror sunglasses. You feel as helpless as a small munchkin trying to play defense against Kareem Abdul-Jabbar. There's no guaranteed way to negotiate yourself out of this, but you can decrease your chances of getting a ticket in this situation.

Initially, get out of your car in a nonthreatening manner. Meet him (sometimes today it's her) with a compliant approach, as if to say, "I'm totally in your hands." Do *not* sit in your vehicle with the windows rolled up. For all he knows, you may be high on drugs or a criminal with a handgun in your lap. Nowadays, some officers get shot by crazies in similar situations. In essence, think of his or her needs and concerns, as well as your own.

While you tender your license, the turning point in this encounter will occur. You have three purposes at this juncture of the interaction:

1. To get his mind off the ticket
2. To have him see you in personal terms
3. To prevent, or at least delay, his pressing his ballpoint pen against the pad of tickets

Start off by saying, "Boy, am I glad *I found you*, officer, because I'm lost! I've been driving around in circles! How do I get to such-and-such a street?"

He'll probably ignore your question for the moment and quickly interject, "Do you realize you were speeding?"

You now steer him back to the question by saying, "Yes, but I'm lost. I don't know where I am!"

The officer will invariably provide directions. While he does this, ask an endless number of subsidiary questions—*anything* to keep him from writing. After he's spent five minutes giving you explicit directions, and you've acted properly grateful, he'll return to the subject at hand—your traffic violation.

At this point, try to make the officer feel important by talking about the danger and difficulty of his job. Portray yourself as a law-abiding citizen, an average working person beset by problems. When he returns to your excessive speed, say, "Gee, I'm sorry. I didn't realize that . . . It was just that I was thinking about . . ." Here, you recount a unique personal dilemma that you confide in him. Everyone has something: a tyrannical boss, a sick spouse, an aged and arthritic parent, an installment payment that can't be met, an unfaithful mate, or a disappointing child.

Make sure you let him know anything else that might bear upon his decision. Assuming you have a record without "blemi," remark, "This will be my first ticket after twelve years of driving. I'd hate to have this tarnish my proud record!" Chances are, he'll hesitate. Cops are reluctant to give anyone a first citation.

Whatever your excuse, it's better if it's unique and different. Keep in mind that this law-enforcement official has practically heard them all. If your saga is special and interesting, it meets his need for some entertainment in what is often a routine and monotonous job. Moreover, he now has a "war story" to recount to his partner or colleagues back at the stationhouse.

Speaking of the uncommon excuse, I was told this story by a police commissioner at the F.B.I. Academy: A policeman was about to ticket a person for driving the wrong way on a one-way street. Suddenly, the accused innocently asked, "Officer, has it occurred to you that the arrow might be pointing in the wrong direction?"

The story teller assured me that this actually happened and that the ticket was never written—presumably as a reward for creativity. As Ripley said, believe it—or not!

Whatever you do, don't remain seated in your car and give the officer a hard time when he queries you. *Never* make "macho" statements like: "So, give me a ticket! I'll fight this all the way to the Supreme Court!"

"I want you to know I'm a person of great wealth and influence."

"Radar's no good, and you know it. Scientifically, your apparatus isn't all that accurate."

Women are probably more effective than men as negotiators in such situations. Statistics show that when a speeding auto is clocked by radar, there is no awareness of the driver's gender. Yet somehow, as a group, women receive about 25 percent fewer citations per thousand drivers than men.

Most women, when stopped, seem to follow the techniques we are outlining. They get out of the car, seem contrite, act friendly, and try to relate to the officer on a human level. I grant you that the 25 percent variation occurred with predominantly male police officers. However, even with the ever-increasing number of females in law enforcement, I don't believe the statistics will change much. Let's face it, in these instances, many women are better at "personalizing."

Let's look at a second example: You are moving from San Jose to San Francisco in six months to reclaim your heart, left there previously. After endless days of looking for a high-rise residence, you learn about a building that is perfect for your family. The problem is that only one apartment will be available, and there are thirty names ahead of yours on the waiting list. You want to go from thirty-first to first on the list. How can you do the seemingly impossible? How can you get what you want?

Go directly to *número uno,* the ultimate decision maker—the building's superintendent. He really is the person with the final say in this matter. Bring your spouse and children with you. Coach the youngsters to behave, and if necessary, resort to "parental bribery." All I am suggesting is reasonable dress, manners, and decorum. There's no need for anyone, children included, to go to an extreme. Put differently, no one expects to rent to a perfect plastic couple named Ken and Barbie.

The point is that you want to appear as a responsible, suitable, stable, and desirable tenant. Keep in mind that the family selected becomes a neighbor of the superintendent, a group that he's stuck with for the duration of the lease. Based on past experience, he knows that the tenants chosen can cause him untold irritation or could conceivably enrich his life. Learn as much as you can about him and his family. At the same time, make sure he sees you in personal, three-dimensional, human terms.

Politely ask to see the apartment that will be available. If he counters with, "I'm sorry, but there are thirty people ahead of you!" don't be deterred. Explain how far you traveled and say in effect, "I know we haven't much of a chance, but can we just get an idea of what it looks like?"

Even if you cannot see that particular flat (it may be occupied), try to get the super to show you any apartment. As a last resort, how about his place? Throughout, you must convey the proper blend of tact, empathy, courtesy, consideration, persistence, affability, and thoughtfulness.

From that day on, whenever you are in the area stop by to visit with the super. Even if he tells you your chances are hopeless, maintain these contacts.

While the superintendent invests considerable chunks of time in you, elaborate on your circumstances, confide in him, and ask him for advice. Detail who you work for, the kind of job you have, the organizations you belong to, the hours you keep, and your interests and hobbies. Do this till the superintendent knows you virtually as well as he knows his own family.

Thanks to your intensive personalizing efforts, what will happen when a vacancy occurs? The superintendent will glance at his list. His eyes will linger on the first name for a moment, but that's all. You see, that name is nothing but a faceless label. He now has the option of renting the apartment to someone he knows nothing about and feels nothing toward . . . or he has the option of renting the apartment to you, about whom he knows plenty. As we said earlier, "The devil known is better than the devil unknown."

Chances are you'll jump from thirty-first place to the top of the list. You'll get that apartment because of the superintendent's investment and his identification with you. You have personalized the selection process. (Of course, this technique will work only where the superintendent has the power to make the selection. In other cases, you will have to make use of other negotiating techniques.)

Now for the third example. When our middle child, Steven, was about to enter his final year of high school, he made extensive summer plans to hitchhike across America. As he put it, "It'll be a great experience, and I won't need much money or clothing."

Needless to say, his parents were totally opposed to this idea. We presented him with the usual objections to such an undertaking: It's physically dangerous; it's illegal in certain areas; and it's unpredictable. After some discussion, he refuted these arguments logically.

Then we came up with what we thought was a sure winner: "Okay," we said, "but no one will give you a ride. People don't pick up hitchhikers any more."

Much to our surprise and dismay, Steven had thought of that problem also. He had purchased a gasoline can from a local filling station, with the intention of cleaning it and transforming the interior into a small dufflebag or suitcase. Apparently, his cross-country trip was not a simple case of teen lunacy, but a goal supported by a well-conceived strategy.

After months of talk and debate, we opted for "benign neglect," allowing him to pursue his dream. When he returned safely, one of the first things he spoke about was the ease of getting lifts from passing vehicles.

Steven remarked that the first driver who stopped for him set the pattern for what was to follow. After proceeding several miles down the road with Steven, the motorist commented, "You walked a hell of a long way to get that gas."

Steven replied, "Oh, I don't own a car. This can is my suitcase. Don't you think it's easier to get rides this way?"

He said that this usually caused guffaws of laughter from the driver, followed by a friendly and informative dialogue.

Although using your thumb as a means of transportation involves considerable risk, it worked well in his case. By carrying that "gasoline can," he personalized himself and distinguished himself from the average hitchhiker. Passing drivers saw him, albeit mistakenly, as a pathetic human being whom they identified with and wanted to help.

Our fourth example: One of the instruments of modern life that enables the individual to be seen as a statistical speck is the computer. Have you ever received an erroneous letter, bill, or statement from a computer? If you have, you know how difficult it is to negotiate with a mechanical thing. You can call and write, but your opponent is programmed to be deaf and blind to your pleas.

How do you get the correction you want?

First, let's deal with a notice you receive in the form of a rectangular computer punch card marked, "Do not fold, tear, or mutilate." Here the solution is simple. Take a pair of scissors or a ballpoint pen and make one or two additional holes in the card. Enjoy yourself and be creative as you violate their injunction, which makes use of the power of legitimacy. Then print the change you desire on the card and mail it back.

When your unique card is put through the system, the computer will reject it, because of the original artwork. A human being will process it by hand. If their records justify the correction you want, it will be made.

Second, let's contend with an erroneous computerized notice in the form of a letter or statement. In this case, call the organization and speak to the person handling your records. In most instances the changes you desire will be forthcoming. Suppose, the same mistake appears the next month? Should this occur, type a "personalized letter" to the individual you spoke with and send a carbon copy to their superior and the top person in the organization. The names of these people can easily be secured from secretaries or telephone operators.

The core of both approaches is to make contact with a

mortal who sees you as a unique human being requiring help.

Continuing to the fifth example: Sharon, our daughter, gets credit for this story. She spent a summer residing with a French family, as part of a student-exchange program. The people she lived with owned a small farm, where they grew melons.

Periodically, they received phone calls from people interested in buying a melon wholesale. In each instance the offer was rejected.

One day, a boy about twelve years old came in person with a similar request. The same answer followed. Nevertheless, the young waif persisted, following the owner around as he did his chores. After listening to the child's personal saga for almost an hour, the farmer paused in the midst of a melon patch.

"Enough!" he said to the boy. "You can have that large one for one franc."

"I only have ten centimes," the boy pleaded.

"Let's see, at that price," the farmer said slyly, winking at Sharon, "how about that little green melon over there?"

"I'll take it," he said. "However, don't cut it off the vine yet. My brother will pick it up in two weeks. You see, I just do the purchasing. He handles shipping and delivery!"

Consider the sixth and final example: Let's say you live in an apartment in a desirable location. It's the middle of January, and you aren't getting enough heat. Even your cat is shivering.

Should you complain to the superintendent, building manager, or landlord? Probably you already have, without getting results. By this time you must realize that I do not believe in approaching anyone in a petulant or aggressive manner. You never "complain," but simply make your needs and circumstances known. Should you come on too strong, the issue shifts from the lack of proper service to your lack of proper manners.

In this example, it is important to determine whether the indoor arctic climate is widespread. Is this a deliberate attempt by the owner to increase his investment return? Should this be the case, all the tenants must get together to act, so as not to suffer the slings and arrows of an outrageous landlord. In essence, utilize the power of commitment.

But let's make this problem more difficult. Somehow you are the only one affected, and you have tried almost everything—phone calls, letters, governmental agencies, and the local radio station's Call for Action—all to no avail!

The situation is very serious, and you have exhausted every reasonable approach. Before you go further, determine who is responsible for this continuing condition. For the sake of argument, we'll say it's an absentee owner.

Now, find out where he lives. Drop in and visit him, unexpectedly, on a Sunday, when his wife and children are present. Act in a concerned, likable, low-key manner. Never accuse him of neglect, because he'll get angry if he loses face in front of his loved ones. Say the equivalent of, "Look—here's my situation. I know you aren't aware of it, because you wouldn't tolerate it. I have a sick child, and the temperature in my unit is only sixty-two degrees. What do you think the problem is— a malfunction or defect in the pipes? What can I do? I *know* you can help me!"

Chances are, on stage, before his family, he won't ignore your plight. Moreover, he no longer knows of you as apartment 203, but rather, sees you as a person with very human needs.

There are no universal prescriptions for every specific negotiation situation. A particular combination of facts exists only at a particular time. But some general principles always apply.

Keep these two things in mind:

1. It's easy for people to shaft others if they don't see them in personal terms.

2. Don't let yourself become a bloodless statistic: a grain of sand that drops through someone's fingers and vanishes in a floor crack. Don't be like Lara in *Dr. Zhivago*, who became "a nameless number on a list that was mislaid." People seldom bother with statistics. Their attitude is: "So, number 463 thinks he has a problem? Who cares?"

Although we have come this far together, a caveat about this approach may be in order. Please recognize that any effective technique carried to an extreme is no longer effective. It may become downright ridiculous. So some moderation is often helpful.

Some time ago I was told an apocryphal story that I would like to share with you. A new priest was so nervous at his first mass, that he could hardly speak. Afterward, he met with his superior, the monsignor, and asked for help.

Pleased by the request, the monsignor placed his arm around the young priest and said, "To hold your audience, you must make the Bible come alive. Your flock must see those times and events as if they were happening today. Remember, Jesus' interest was in the redemption of man's very humanity. His mission was not to govern men, but to release them.

"In other words," the monsignor said, leaning closer, "make it a personal experience for the worshipers. Use their language. Tell it like it is, as the young people say."

The priest was nodding enthusiastically, encouraging his superior to continue.

Impressed by the attitude of the young man, the monsignor couldn't resist one last piece of experienced advice. Beckoning the priest closer, he whispered, "Oh, yes—it might help you relax a little if you put some vodka or gin in your water glass."

The next Sunday, following his superior's instructions to the letter, the young priest was very much at ease and talked up a storm. However, he noticed the monsignor, in the rear of the congregation, furiously taking notes.

When the mass was over he rushed up to his superior, anxious for some more sagacious feedback. "Well, how did I do this week?"

"Fine" the monsignor said, "but there are six things that you might straighten out in the future."

He then handed the priest his notes, which follow:

1. They are the Ten Commandments, not "the top ten on the charts."
2. There were twelve disciples, not "a whole gross."
3. David slew Goliath. He did not "whip his ass."
4. We do not refer to Jesus Christ as "the late J.C."
5. Next Sunday there is a taffy-pulling contest at St. Peter's, not "a peter-pulling contest at St. Taffy's."
6. The Father, Son, and Holy Ghost are not referred to as "Big Daddy, Junior, and the Spook."

Moral: Don't be a literalist. Do what is appropriate under the circumstances—exercising moderation always.

Probably, one of the most effective uses of "personalizing power" was made by the late Richard J. Daley, long-time mayor of Chicago. Let me try to contrast and characterize his approach with a contemporary in big-city government, John Lindsay, New York City's former mayor.

In my opinion, John Lindsay was the best-looking mayor the Big Apple ever had. Lean, chisel featured, and square jawed, he could easily have pursued a career in media or show business. He was the tallest mayor the city ever had—which isn't saying much. His dress was impeccable; he was an eloquent speaker. Why, he didn't even sound as if he came from New York. This, if nothing else, should have qualified him to be the mayor of New York. John Lindsay appeared to have everything.

Did John Lindsay, a decent public servant with the best intentions, achieve his objectives? Not at all. Why not? Because despite his engaging personality he didn't personalize. He always negotiated on behalf of the City of New York. He said such things as, "New York City would like you to honor your commitment." Do you think people like labor leader Michael Quill (who played the "dumb is better" routine by always mispronouncing the mayor's name as "Lindsley") cared about this impersonal abstraction? The megalopolis of New York is too big for a finite mind to comprehend. To Quill it was like a request from the British Empire.

Daley, on the other hand, was short, with a silly-putty body. When he lost weight he could best be described as pudgy. He clothed himself in suits that had been out of style for thirty years. When he spoke publicly his syntax butchered the English language.

One day he would cut the ribbon on a new school and dedicate the building to the "highest platitudes of learning." Thereafter, he would defend an indicted crony with, "We've been boyhood friends all our lives," and then dismiss the Vietnam War protest by remarking, "I don't see any more serious division in our country than we had during the Civil War." He once advised a group of business executives, "Today, the real problem is the future."

Then there was his famous rebuttal to reports of a police riot during the demonstrations at the Democratic National Convention in 1968. "The police are not here to create disorder," he said. "They are here to *preserve disorder!*"

When the newspapers dutifully quoted him, Earl Bush, his press secretary, blamed the media.

"It's damn bad reporting," he told the reporters gathered. "You should have quoted what the mayor meant, not what he said." (Somehow they understood that.) "Hizzoner" himself even reproached the press: "You have condemned me, you have vilified me, you have even criticized me."

Were Daley's appearance and garbled speech a drawback?
To the contrary. They made him human, endearing, and ap-
pealing. He's still so revered in Chicago that you might say
he's on the verge of local canonization.

Late last autumn I was sitting in a plane at O'Hare waiting
to depart. My seatmate asked, "Is it snowing outside?" After
glancing out the window I assured him that it was. He responded matter of factly, "You know, when Daley was alive,
it never snowed this early!"

The late mayor is buried in an unimpressive grave site at
a small cemetery in Chicago. However, year in and year out,
tens of thousands of visitors make a pilgrimage to his last
resting-place, to pay homage. As a matter of fact, the weight
of all these people has caused the ground to sink around the
grave, and the mound of earth, under which his remains lie,
has risen. Why does this multitude come? For all we know,
they're still asking for favors. And for all we know, he's still
granting them!

Why is it that even today, management and business people in Chicago claim, "Daley was our friend; he *really* understood business"? Why do labor representatives still say, "Daley
really understood the working man and his needs!" How
could he possibly deal with both sides of the fence, then convince each group he was on *its* side? Because unlike Lindsay,
Daley negotiated *personally*. He never negotiated on behalf
of the Democratic National Committee, the Democratic party,
or the City of Chicago. He knew in his gut that such concepts
were too abstract. Instead, he approached individuals privately, one by one, asking for their commitment to him personally.

For instance, he'd say the equivalent of: "John . . . you
told me you were gonna do this. I was *counting* on you.
I told my wife about your promise. You can't let me down!
Do you know that I include you in my prayers when I say my
rosary? I even lit a candle for you this morning! Look . . .
here's the wax on my fingers!"

That's "personalizing power"!

Now that we have come full circle, I trust that the end of this journey marks the beginning of a rewarding and liberating phase of your life.

You have a role to play in this world—a reason for being here. But it is up to you to find your part and direct your future.

You alone determine your destiny through your own efforts. Accept this responsibility—not just for yourself, but for us all. You have the power to change your life and the lives of others as well. Don't back away from the exercise of power or wait for someone else to act. Of course you can get what you want, but part of what you want should be to help others along the way.

The good life is not a passive existence where you live and let live. It is one of involvement where you live and help live.

Allow me to close this book with words written by William Styron in *Sophie's Choice*:

> The most profound statement yet made about Auschwitz was not a statement at all, but a response.
> The query: "At Auschwitz, tell me, where was God?"
> And the answer: "Where was man?"

ABOUT THE AUTHOR

For the past three decades, HERB COHEN has been a participant in thousands of negotiations. These have included every situation imaginable, from mergers and acquisitions to hostage and terrorist negotiations for law-enforcement agencies.

Herb Cohen is a consultant to some of the largest corporations and governmental agencies in North America. In addition, he travels internationally to conferences and conventions, where his entertaining and informative style makes him a sought-after speaker.

Through the years, Cohen has shared his proven techniques with thousands of business people, government leaders, and professionals who've attended his successful seminars on Power Negotiations®. And *successful* is the right word for Herb Cohen. Despite a hectic schedule that keeps him on the road more than 200 days a year, he manages to teach at top educational institutions, such as Harvard University, the University of Michigan, The Brookings Institution, and the F.B.I. Academy.